CliffsNotes™

Shakespeare's
Romeo and Juliet

By Annaliese F. Connolly

IN THIS BOOK

- Learn about the Life and Background of the Playwright
- Preview an Introduction to the Play
- Explore themes, character development, and recurring images in Critical Commentaries
- Examine in-depth Character Analyses
- Acquire an understanding of the play with Critical Essays
- Reinforce what you learn with CliffsNotes Review
- Find additional information to further your study in CliffsNotes Resource Center and online at www.cliffsnotes.com

Hungry Minds™

Best-Selling Books • Digital Downloads • e-Books • Answer Networks • e-Newsletters • Branded Web Sites • e-Learning
New York, NY • Cleveland, OH • Indianapolis, IN

About the Author

Annaliese Connolly is a graduate of Sheffield Hallam University and is currently pursuing her Ph.D. degree in Renaissance drama.

Publisher's Acknowledgments

Editorial

Project Editor: Keith Peterson
Acquisitions Editor: Greg Tubach
Copy Editor: Janet M. Withers
Editorial Assistant: Carol Strickland
Glossary Editors: The editors and staff of Webster's New World Dictionaries

Production

Indexer: York Production Services, Inc.
Proofreader: York Production Services, Inc.
Hungry Minds Indianapolis Production Services

Distributed by CDG Books Canada Inc. for Canada; by Transworld Publishers Limited in the United Kingdom; by IDG Norge Books for Norway; by IDG Sweden Books for Sweden; by IDG Books Australia Publishing Corporation Pty. Ltd. for Australia and New Zealand; by TransQuest Publishers Pte Ltd. for Singapore, Malaysia, Thailand, Indonesia, and Hong Kong; by Gotop Information Inc. for Taiwan; by ICG Muse, Inc. for Japan; by Norma Comunicaciones S.A. for Columbia; by Intersoft for South Africa; by Eyrolles for France; by International Thomson Publishing for Germany, Austria and Switzerland; by Distribuidora Cuspide for Argentina; by LR International for Brazil; by Galileo Libros for Chile; by Ediciones ZETA S.C.R. Ltda. for Peru; by WS Computer Publishing Corporation, Inc., for the Philippines; by Contemporanea de Ediciones for Venezuela; by Express Computer Distributors for the Caribbean and West Indies; by Micronesia Media Distributor, Inc. for Micronesia; by Grupo Editorial Norma S.A. for Guatemala; by Chips Computadoras S.A. de C.V. for Mexico; by Editorial Norma de Panama S.A. for Panama; by American Bookshops for Finland. Authorized Sales Agent: Anthony Rudkin Associates for the Middle East and North Africa.

For general information on Hungry Minds' products and services please contact our Customer Care department; within the U.S. at 800-762-2974, outside the U.S. at 317-572-3993 or fax 317-572-4002.

For sales inquiries and resellers information, including discounts, premium and bulk quantity sales and foreign language translations please contact our Customer Care department at 800-434-3422, fax 317-572-4002 or write to Hungry Minds, Inc., Attn: Customer Care department, 10475 Crosspoint Boulevard, Indianapolis, IN 46256.

For information on licensing foreign or domestic rights, please contact our Sub-Rights Customer Care department at 212-884-5000.

For information on using Hungry Minds' products and services in the classroom or for ordering examination copies, please contact our Educational Sales department at 800-434-2086 or fax 317-572-4005.

Please contact our Public Relations department at 212-884-5163 for press review copies or 212-884-5000 for author interviews and other publicity information or fax 212-884-5400.

For authorization to photocopy items for corporate, personal, or educational use, please contact Copyright Clearance Center, 222 Rosewood Drive, Danvers, MA 01923, or fax 978-750-4470.

LIMIT OF LIABILITY/DISCLAIMER OF WARRANTY: THE PUBLISHER AND AUTHOR HAVE USED THEIR BEST EFFORTS IN PREPARING THIS BOOK. THE PUBLISHER AND AUTHOR MAKE NO REPRESENTATIONS OR WARRANTIES WITH RESPECT TO THE ACCURACY OR COMPLETENESS OF THE CONTENTS OF THIS BOOK AND SPECIFICALLY DISCLAIM ANY IMPLIED WARRANTIES OF MERCHANTABILITY OR FITNESS FOR A PARTICULAR PURPOSE. THERE ARE NO WARRANTIES WHICH EXTEND BEYOND THE DESCRIPTIONS CONTAINED IN THIS PARAGRAPH. NO WARRANTY MAY BE CREATED OR EXTENDED BY SALES REPRESENTATIVES OR WRITTEN SALES MATERIALS. THE ACCURACY AND COMPLETENESS OF THE INFORMATION PROVIDED HEREIN AND THE OPINIONS STATED HEREIN ARE NOT GUARANTEED OR WARRANTED TO PRODUCE ANY PARTICULAR RESULTS, AND THE ADVICE AND STRATEGIES CONTAINED HEREIN MAY NOT BE SUITABLE FOR EVERY INDIVIDUAL. NEITHER THE PUBLISHER NOR AUTHOR SHALL BE LIABLE FOR ANY LOSS OF PROFIT OR ANY OTHER COMMERCIAL DAMAGES, INCLUDING BUT NOT LIMITED TO SPECIAL, INCIDENTAL, CONSEQUENTIAL, OR OTHER DAMAGES. FULFILLMENT OF EACH COUPON OFFER IS THE RESPONSIBILITY OF THE OFFEROR.

Trademarks: Cliffs, CliffsNotes, the CliffsNotes logo, CliffsAP, CliffsComplete, CliffsTestPrep, CliffsQuickReview, CliffsNote-a-Day and all related logos and trade dress are registered trademarks or trademarks of Hungry Minds, Inc., in the United States and other countries. All other trademarks are property of their respective owners. Hungry Minds, Inc., is not associated with any product or vendor mentioned in this book.

Hungry Minds⁻ is a trademark of Hungry Minds, Inc.

Table of Contents

How to Use This Book

CliffsNotes on Shakespeare's *Romeo and Juliet* supplements the original work, giving you background information about the author, an introduction to the play, a graphical character map, critical commentaries, expanded glossaries, and a comprehensive index. CliffsNotes Review tests your comprehension of the original text and reinforces learning with questions and answers, practice projects, and more. For further information on William Shakespeare and *Romeo and Juliet*, check out the CliffsNotes Resource Center.

CliffsNotes provides the following icons to highlight essential elements of particular interest:

Reveals the underlying themes in the work.

Helps you to more easily relate to or discover the depth of a character.

Uncovers elements such as setting, atmosphere, mystery, passion, violence, irony, symbolism, tragedy, foreshadowing, and satire.

Enables you to appreciate the nuances of words and phrases.

Don't Miss Our Web Site

Discover classic literature as well as modern-day treasures by visiting the CliffsNotes Web site at www.cliffsnotes.com. You can obtain a quick download of a CliffsNotes title, purchase a title in print form, browse our catalog, or view online samples.

You'll also find interactive tools that are fun and informative, links to interesting Web sites, tips, articles, and additional resources to help you, not only for literature, but for test prep, finance, careers, computers, and Internet too. See you at www.cliffsnotes.com!

LIFE AND BACKGROUND OF THE PLAYWRIGHT

Personal Background

Many scholars have speculated about the life and career of William Shakespeare. People interested in studying England's foremost dramatic poet need to distinguish between *facts* and *beliefs* about his life. Sparse and scattered as facts of his life are, they are sufficient to prove that a man from Stratford by the name of William Shakespeare wrote the major portion of the 37 plays that scholars ascribe to him. This concise review covers some of these records and some speculations about his life.

William Shakespeare was born on April 23, 1564, in Stratford-upon-Avon in England. His baptism occurred on Wednesday, April 26, 1564 (this is in keeping with the usual Elizabethan practice of baptizing children three days after their birth). His father was John Shakespeare, tanner, glover, dealer in grain, and town official of Stratford. His mother, Mary, was the daughter of Robert Arden, a prosperous gentleman-farmer. The family lived on Henley Street. Recent research into John Shakespeare's life suggests that Shakespeare was raised Catholic. As the son of a local businessman, Shakespeare probably attended King's New School, the local grammar school, where he received a good education. There is evidence that due to his father's declining fortunes, Shakespeare was unable to complete his schooling and was subsequently required to help with the family business.

Under a bond dated November 28, 1582, William Shakespeare and Anne Hathaway were married. Much speculation has arisen as to the happiness of that marriage, and it is widely thought that Shakespeare may have been forced to marry Anne Hathaway because she was pregnant. The birth of their daughter, Susanna, six months later, supports this theory. Researchers have also noted that Shakespeare left Hathaway his "second best bed" in his will as evidence of their unhappy marriage. Susanna's baptism took place in Stratford in May 1583. One year and nine months later, their twins, Hamnet and Judith (named after the poet's friends Hamnet and Judith Sadler), were christened in the same church. Hamnet died in 1596 at age eleven.

The years between 1585-1592 are referred to as "the seven lost years" because we have few records of Shakespeare's life during this period. The absence of any factual information makes these years a rich source of speculation. Some speculate that Shakespeare may have been a soldier for a time. Much of this theory is based upon evidence from his plays and the attention he gives to the themes of corruption in the army in *Henry IV*, parts 1 and 2 and *Henry V*. Recent research has suggested that Shakespeare left Stratford for Lancashire in northern England.

There, he may have worked as an actor and tutor in a noble household. Eventually, he traveled to London with his fellow actors.

Early in 1596, William Shakespeare, in his father's name, applied to the College of Heralds for a coat of arms. Although positive proof is lacking, the Heralds most likely granted this request, for in 1599, Shakespeare again made application for the right to quarter his coat of arms with that of his mother. Entitled to her father's coat of arms, Mary had lost this privilege when she married John Shakespeare before he held the official status of gentleman. This evidence suggests that Shakespeare was now a wealthy man who wanted social recognition of his status.

In May 1597, Shakespeare purchased New Place, the outstanding residential property in Stratford at that time. Since John Shakespeare had suffered financial reverses prior to this date, William must have achieved success for himself.

Court records show that in 1601-02, Shakespeare began rooming in the household of Christopher Mountjoy in London. Subsequent disputes over a wedding settlement and agreement between Mountjoy and his son-in-law, Stephen Belott, led to a series of legal actions, and in 1612, the court scribe recorded Shakespeare's deposition of testimony relating to the case.

In July 1605, Shakespeare paid 440 pounds for the lease of a large portion of the tithes, or taxes, on certain real estate in and near Stratford. This was an arrangement whereby Shakespeare purchased half the annual tithes on certain agricultural products from parcels of land in and near Stratford. In addition to receiving approximately 10 percent income on his investment, he almost doubled his capital. This was possibly the most important and successful investment of his lifetime, and it paid a steady income for many years.

Shakespeare is next mentioned when John Combe, a resident of Stratford, died on July 12, 1614 and bequeathed 5 pounds to his friend. Such records are important, not for their economic significance but because they prove the existence of a William Shakespeare in Stratford and in London during this period.

On March 25, 1616, William Shakespeare revised his last will and testament. He died on April 23 of the same year. His body lies within the chancel and before the altar of the collegiate church of the Holy Trinity in Stratford. A rather wry inscription is carved upon his tombstone:

Good Friend, for Jesus' sake, forbear
To dig the dust enclosed here;

Blest be the man that spares these stones,
And curst be he who moves my bones.

The last direct descendant of William Shakespeare was his grand-daughter, Elizabeth Hall, who died in 1670.

Career Highlights

The evidence establishing William Shakespeare as the foremost playwright of his day is also positive and persuasive. For example, Robert Greene's *Groatsworth of Wit*, in which he attacked Shakespeare, a mere actor, for presuming to write plays in competition with Greene and his fellow playwrights, was entered in the Stationers' Register on September 20, 1592.

Shakespeare was the resident writer for the Lord Chamberlain's Men, who were based at the playhouse called the Theatre in Shoreditch, in London. In 1594, Shakespeare acted before Queen Elizabeth, and records suggest that Shakespeare played the role of the Ghost in *Hamlet* and William in *As You Like It*. In 1594 and 1595, his name appeared as one of the shareholders of the Lord Chamberlain's Company. Francis Meres, in his *Palladis Tamia* (1598), called Shakespeare "mellifluous and hony-tongued" and compared his comedies and tragedies with those of Plautus and Seneca (respected classical playwrights) in excellence.

Shakespeare's association with Richard Burbage's acting company is equally definite. His name appears as one of the owners of the Globe Theatre in 1599. On May 19, 1603, he and his fellow actors received a patent from James I designating them as the King's Men and making them Grooms of the Chamber. Late in 1608 or early in 1609, Shakespeare and his colleagues purchased the Blackfriars Theatre and began using it as their winter location when weather made production at the Globe inconvenient.

One of the most impressive of all proofs of Shakespeare's authorship of his plays is the First Folio of 1623, with the dedicatory verse that appeared in it. John Heminge and Henry Condell, members of Shakespeare's own company, stated that they collected and issued the plays as a memorial to their fellow actor. Many contemporary poets contributed eulogies to Shakespeare; one of the best known of these poems is by Ben Jonson, a fellow actor and, later, a friendly rival. Jonson also criticized Shakespeare's dramatic work in *Timber: or, Discoveries* (1641).

INTRODUCTION
TO THE PLAY

Date of Composition

Shakespeare wrote *Romeo and Juliet* early in his career, between 1594-1595, around the same time as the comedies *Love's Labour's Lost* and *A Midsummer Night's Dream*. Scholars often group these plays together because they explore the themes of love, courtship, and marriage. The plays also share a similar poetic quality in the language used, as they incorporate sonnets and the conventions associated with them such as falling in love at first sight.

First Performance

The first performance of *Romeo and Juliet* took place in the autumn/winter of 1594, when the playhouses reopened for the first time after a sustained outbreak of the plague had forced the authorities to close all the playhouses in London in January 1593. During this period, over 10,000 people in London alone died from the disease, and Shakespeare emphasizes the relevance of the plague for his audience by using it in *Romeo and Juliet* to prevent Friar Laurence's message from reaching Romeo in Mantua.

The first performance of the play was at the playhouse called the Theatre where Shakespeare and his company the Lord Chamberlain's Men were based until 1597. The Theatre was the first purpose-built playhouse in London and could hold over 1,500 people. It was a large, octagonal-shaped building with a thatched roof just around the perimeter so that the yard below was open air. Most of the audience, referred to as *groundlings,* paid a penny to stand in the yard surrounding the stage. Wealthier playgoers preferred to pay an extra penny to sit in one of the galleries so that they could watch the play in comfort and more importantly, be seen by the rest of the audience.

In the first performance of *Romeo and Juliet,* Richard Burbage, the company's leading actor, who was in his mid-twenties, played Romeo. Juliet was played by Master Robert Goffe; young boy actors often played female roles because women did not legally appear on the stage until the late 17th century.

Cultural Influences

During the 16th century, many English dramatists and poets adapted a wide range of Italian stories and poetry to create their own material. The availability of these sources reflects the English interest in Italian culture during this period as the influence of the Italian Renaissance spread. The term *Renaissance* means "rebirth" and refers to the period after the Middle Ages when a revival of interest in classical Roman and Greek culture emerged. Beginning in the mid-14th century in Italy, the Renaissance was a period of rapid discovery and development, gradually moving northwards across the rest of Europe.

One Italian source that Shakespeare draws upon in *Romeo and Juliet* is Francesco Petrarch, 1304-1374, an Italian scholar and poet, who was responsible for developing the sonnet. The poems, which Petrarch wrote for the lady he admired, describe the process of falling in love and courtship, according to medieval ideas of courtly love and chivalry. Translated into English and published in 1557, the sonnets were extremely popular, so English sonnet writers imitated and developed Petrarch's conventions.

A sonnet is a poem made up of 14 lines of iambic pentameter. That is, each line consists of ten syllables with a regular rhyme scheme. Both the prologues to Act I and Act II in *Romeo and Juliet*, as well as Romeo and Juliet's first exchanges in Act I, Scene 5, are sonnets. The sonnet can be traced by identifying the rhyme at the end of each line, starting, for example, with Romeo's line: "If I profane with my unworthiest hand" down to: "Then move not, while my prayer's effect I take." The first rhyming line may be called A and the second B, until the pattern ABAB CDCD EFEF GG is completed.

In *Romeo and Juliet,* Shakespeare presents the Prologue as a sonnet in order to point to the play's themes of love and the feud because sonnets were often used to address the subject of love in conflict. The sonnet also draws on the audience's expectations of the kinds of imagery that will be used. In his sonnets, Petrarch established the following pattern for love: A young man falls in love at first sight with a beautiful woman, but the woman resists his love in order to prolong the courtship and test his devotion. This results in the lover becoming melancholy, avoiding his friends and family, and using poetry to express his feelings of rejection. In the opening scenes of the play, Romeo is presented as a typical Petrarchan lover, rejected by Rosaline, the lady he admires. Romeo uses artificial-sounding language to describe his emotions: "Love is a smoke made with the fume of sighs." Shakespeare continues to use the Petrarchan model when Romeo and Juliet fall in love at first sight at the Capulet ball. In this instance, Romeo realizes that his love for Rosaline was blind: "Did my heart love till now? Forswear it, sight. / For I ne'er saw true beauty till this night."

Shakespeare's Adaptation of Brooke's *The Tragical Historye of Romeus and Juliet*

Shakespeare's audience already knew the essential story of Romeo and Juliet, a popular story in European folklore which Arthur Brooke had translated into English in 1562 as a poem called *The Tragicall Historye of Romeus and Juliet*. Brooke based his poem on Pierre Boaistuau's French translation of the story from Italian sources in 1559.

Shakespeare adapts Brooke's poem for the stage, developing the characters, condensing the timeframe, and adding certain scenes to underscore his own themes. For example, Shakespeare reduces Juliet's age from 16 to 13 to emphasize her youth and vulnerability. Shakespeare expands Mercutio's role by adding the scenes in which Mercutio gives his Queen Mab speech and meets the Nurse. Shakespeare also develops the scene in which Romeo kills Tybalt: First, Mercutio accepts Tybalt's challenge on Romeo's behalf, and then Tybalt kills Mercutio under Romeo's arm as he tries to part the two men. In Brooke, Romeo kills Tybalt in self-defense, but Shakespeare shifts the emphasis so that Romeo is forced to take revenge for his friend's death by killing Tybalt.

Shakespeare compresses the action from months, as it appears in Brooke, to just over four days. In Brooke, Romeo and Juliet have been married nearly three months before Tybalt's death brings about their separation. In Shakespeare's play, Romeo and Juliet's wedding occurs on the same day as Romeo's banishment, so that the lovers are only able to spend a single night together. Shakespeare also develops the plot by adding the scene in which Capulet brings the wedding forward from Thursday to Wednesday. These developments are used to indicate the speed with which Romeo and Juliet rush headlong into love, while creating intense pressure as events conspire to bring the lovers to their tragic deaths.

A Brief Synopsis

Day 1 - Sunday: Act I, Scene 1–Act II, Scene 2

As the play begins, a long-standing feud between the Montague and Capulet families continues to disrupt the peace of Verona, a city in northern Italy. A brawl between the servants of the feuding households prompts the Prince to threaten both sides to keep the peace on pain of death.

Benvolio advises his lovesick friend Romeo, (son of Montague), to abandon his unrequited love for Rosaline and seek another.

That night, Capulet holds a masked ball to encourage a courtship between his daughter, Juliet, and Paris, a relative of the Prince. Concealing their identities behind masks, Romeo and Benvolio go to the ball, where Romeo and Juliet fall in love at first sight, but at the end of the evening discover their identities as members of the opposed families. On his way home from the feast, Romeo climbs into Capulet's orchard to glimpse Juliet again. Juliet appears at her balcony, and the couple exchange vows of love, agreeing to marry the next day.

Day 2 - Monday   Act II, Scene 3 – Act III, Scene 4

Romeo asks Friar Laurence to perform the marriage ceremony. Though initially reluctant, he finally agrees, hoping to reconcile the families, and marries Romeo and Juliet that afternoon.

Meanwhile, Tybalt, Juliet's cousin, sends Romeo a challenge to a duel. Romeo refuses to fight when Tybalt confronts him because they're now related. However, Mercutio, Romeo's quick-tempered friend, intervenes and accepts the challenge. Romeo tries to part the other two as they fight, but Mercutio is fatally wounded under Romeo's arm. To avenge Mercutio's death, Romeo kills Tybalt and then flees.

The Prince announces Romeo's banishment for Tybalt's murder. Romeo, in hiding at the Friar's cell, becomes hysterical at the news of his sentence and tries to kill himself, but the Friar promises to make Romeo's marriage to Juliet public and gain the Prince's pardon. Romeo and Juliet celebrate their wedding night before he leaves at dawn for Mantua.

Day 3 - Tuesday   Act III, Scene 5 – Act IV, Scene 3

That morning, Juliet discovers that her father has arranged for her to marry Paris on Thursday. The Capulets, unaware that Juliet is grieving for Romeo's exile rather than Tybalt's death, believe the wedding will distract her from mourning. Distressed at the prospect of a false marriage and isolated from her family, Juliet seeks advice from Friar Laurence, who offers her a sleeping potion to make her appear dead for 42 hours. During this time, the Friar will send a message to Romeo in Mantua so that Romeo can return to Verona in time for Juliet to awake.

Juliet returns home and agrees to marry Paris. In a moment of euphoria, Capulet brings the wedding forward from Thursday to

Wednesday, thereby forcing Juliet to take the potion that night and reducing the time for the message to reach Romeo.

Day 4 - Wednesday   **Act IV, Scene 4 – Act V, Scene 2**

Early on Wednesday morning, Juliet's seemingly lifeless body is discovered and she is placed in the family tomb. Because an outbreak of the plague prevents the Friar's messenger from leaving Verona, Romeo now receives news of Juliet's death instead. Desperate, Romeo buys poison from an apothecary and returns to Verona.

Late that night, Romeo enters the Capulet tomb, but is confronted by Paris, whom he fights and kills.

Still unaware that Juliet is in fact alive, Romeo takes the poison and dies. The Friar, arriving too late, discovers the bodies as Juliet begins to stir. He begs her to leave with him, but Juliet refuses, and then stabs herself with Romeo's dagger.

Day 5 - Thursday: **Act V, Scene 3**

As dawn breaks, the Watch arrives, closely followed by the Prince, who demands a full inquiry into what has happened. The two families then arrive, and the Friar comes forward to explain the tragic sequence of events. The deaths of Romeo and Juliet finally bring the feud to an end as Montague and Capulet join hands in peace.

List Of Characters

Juliet Capulet's daughter. She is presented as a young and innocent adolescent, not yet 14 years old. Her youthfulness is stressed throughout the play to illustrate her progression from adolescence to maturity and to emphasize her position as a tragic heroine. Juliet's love for Romeo gives her the strength and courage to defy her parents and face death twice.

Romeo Montague's son, who is loved and respected in Verona. He is initially presented as a comic lover, with his inflated declarations of love for Rosaline. After meeting Juliet, he abandons his tendency to be a traditional, fashionable lover, and his language becomes intense, reflecting his genuine passion for Juliet. By avenging Mercutio's death, he sets in motion a chain of tragic events that culminate in suicide when he mistakenly believes Juliet to be dead.

Mercutio Kinsman to the prince and friend of Romeo. His name comes from the word *mercury,* the element which indicates his quick temper. Mercutio is bawdy, talkative, and tries to tease Romeo out of his melancholy frame of mind. He accepts Tybalt's challenge to defend Romeo's honor and is killed, thus precipitating Romeo's enraged reaction during which Romeo kills Tybalt.

Tybalt Lady Capulet's nephew and Juliet's cousin. Tybalt is violent and hot-tempered, with a strong sense of honor. He challenges Romeo to a duel in response to Romeo's attending a Capulet party. His challenge to Romeo is taken up by Mercutio, whom Tybalt kills. Romeo then kills Tybalt.

The Nurse Juliet's nursemaid, who acts as confidante and messenger for Romeo and Juliet. Like Mercutio, the Nurse loves to talk and reminisce, and her attitude toward love is bawdy. The Nurse is loving and affectionate toward Juliet, but compromises her position of trust when she advises Juliet to forget Romeo and comply with her parents' wishes and marry Paris.

Friar Laurence A brother of the Franciscan order and Romeo's confessor, who advises both Romeo and Juliet. The Friar agrees to marry the couple in secret in the hope that marriage will restore peace between their families. His plans to reunite Juliet with Romeo are thwarted by the influence of fate. The Friar concocts the potion plot through which Juliet appears dead for 42 hours in order to avoid marrying Paris. At the end of the play, the Prince recognizes the Friar's good intentions.

Capulet Juliet's father is quick-tempered and impetuous but is initially reluctant to consent to Juliet's marriage with Paris because Juliet is so young. Later, he changes his mind and angrily demands that Juliet obey his wishes. The deaths of Romeo and Juliet reconcile Capulet and Montague.

Paris A noble young kinsman to the Prince. Paris is well-mannered and attractive and hopes to marry Juliet. Romeo fights and kills Paris at the Capulet tomb when Paris thinks that Romeo has come to desecrate the bodes of Tybalt and Juliet.

Benvolio Montague's nephew and friend of Romeo and Mercutio. Benvolio is the peacemaker who attempts to keep peace between Tybalt and Mercutio. After the deaths of Mercutio and Tybalt, Benvolio acts as a Chorus, explaining how events took place.

Lady Capulet Lady Capulet is vengeful and she demands Romeo's death for killing Tybalt. In her relationship with Juliet, she is cold and distant, expecting Juliet to obey her father and marry Paris.

Montague Romeo's father, who is concerned by his son's melancholy behavior.

Balthasar Romeo's servant. He brings Romeo the news in Mantua that Juliet is dead.

An Apothecary A poverty-stricken chemist, who illegally sells poison to Romeo.

Escalus, Prince of Verona The symbol of law and order in Verona, but he fails to prevent further outbreaks of the violence between the Montagues and Capulets. Only the deaths of Romeo and Juliet, rather than the authority of the prince, restore peace.

Friar John A brother of the Franciscan order, sent by Friar Laurence to tell Romeo of his sleeping potion plan for Juliet. The Friar is prevented from getting to Mantua and the message does not reach Romeo.

Lady Montague In contrast with Lady Capulet, Lady Montague is peace-loving and dislikes the violence of the feud. Like her husband, she is concerned by her son's withdrawn and secretive behavior. The news of Romeo's banishment breaks her heart, and she dies of grief.

Peter A Capulet servant attending the Nurse.

Abram A servant to Montague.

Sampson Servant of the Capulet household.

Gregory Servant of the Capulet household.

Character Map

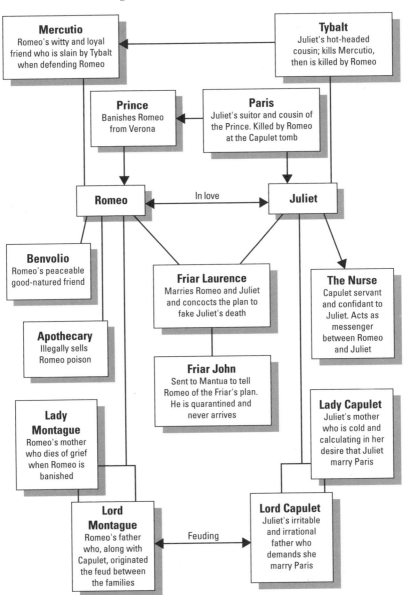

Mercutio
Romeo's witty and loyal friend who is slain by Tybalt when defending Romeo

Tybalt
Juliet's hot-headed cousin; kills Mercutio, then is killed by Romeo

Prince
Banishes Romeo from Verona

Paris
Juliet's suitor and cousin of the Prince. Killed by Romeo at the Capulet tomb

Romeo

In love

Juliet

Benvolio
Romeo's peaceable good-natured friend

Friar Laurence
Marries Romeo and Juliet and concocts the plan to fake Juliet's death

The Nurse
Capulet servant and confidant to Juliet. Acts as messenger between Romeo and Juliet

Apothecary
Illegally sells Romeo poison

Friar John
Sent to Mantua to tell Romeo of the Friar's plan. He is quarantined and never arrives

Lady Capulet
Juliet's mother who is cold and calculating in her desire that Juliet marry Paris

Lady Montague
Romeo's mother who dies of grief when Romeo is banished

Lord Montague
Romeo's father who, along with Capulet, originated the feud between the families

Feuding

Lord Capulet
Juliet's irritable and irrational father who demands she marry Paris

CRITICAL COMMENTARIES

Prologue

The Chorus, often played by a single narrator, opens *Romeo and Juliet* with a brief summary of what's to come on stage. Just as the Chorus in ancient Greek tragedies provided a commentary on events in the play for the audience, so Shakespeare's Chorus sets the scene for tragedy by presenting his two young protagonists as the victims of fate whose lives are marred from the outset by the feud between their families: "From forth the fatal loins of these two foes / A pair of star-cross'd lovers take their life." Any lack of suspense as to the outcome of the play serves to emphasize the major theme of fate—an omnipresent force looming over Romeo and Juliet's "death-marked" love.

The prologue is also a sonnet, a popular form of 16th-century love poem that often explored such themes as love in conflict. Shakespeare chooses this poetic form to outline the play's main issues of love and feuding and to present another major theme: how true love ultimately triumphs because the deaths of Romeo and Juliet end the feud between their families.

Glossary

dignity rank, or title.

fatal loins fateful, unfortunate, offspring.

star-cross'd lovers lovers destined to an unhappy fate.

misadventur'd unlucky.

piteous overthrows their end or death, which arouses or deserves pity or compassion.

death-mark'd doomed from the outset; fated.

two hours traffic the usual duration of a play.

ACT I
Scene 1

Summary

The scene opens with a brawl on the streets of Verona between servants from the affluent Montague and Capulet households. While
attempting to stop the fight, Benvolio (Romeo's cousin) is drawn into
the fray by Tybalt, kinsman of the Capulets. The fight rapidly escalates
as more citizens become involved and soon the heads of both households appear on the scene. At last, Prince Escalus arrives and stops the
riot, forbidding any further outbreaks of violence on pain of death.

After Escalus dismisses both sides, Montague and his wife discuss
Romeo's recent melancholy behavior with Benvolio and ask him to discover its cause. They exit as Romeo enters in his sad state—a victim of
an unrequited love for the cold and unresponsive Rosaline. Benvolio
advises him to forget Rosaline by looking for another, but Romeo insists
that this would be impossible.

Commentary

A spirited exchange of vulgar jokes between servants opens the play
and immediately links sex with conflict. In their bawdy quarrel, the servants' references to "tool" and "naked weapon," together with repeated
images of striking and thrusting, illustrate how images of love and sex
are intertwined with violence and death—and will continue to be
throughout the play.

The sudden switch from the comedic interplay between the servants
to a potentially life-threatening situation demonstrates the rapidly
changing pace that drives the action of the rest of the play. For instance,
Benvolio, whose name means "goodwill," tries to act as a peacemaker
by dividing the servants, but the quick-tempered "fiery Tybalt" forces
him to draw his sword, and the atmosphere changes from harmony to
hatred within a few lines. This undercurrent of uncertain fortune
wrenches the characters into and out of pleasure and pain as fate seemingly preempts each of their hopes with another tragic turn of events.

When the elderly, hot-tempered Capulet calls for his long sword to jump into a duel with the young swordsmen wielding light, modern weapons, both the absurdity of the feud and the gulf between the old and the young are evident. Both patriarchs are chastised by their wives for such impetuous behavior: "A crutch. Why call you for a sword?" chides Capulet's wife. Though Romeo and Juliet try to separate themselves from such archaic grudges and foolish fighting, the couple can't escape the repercussions of the feud, which ultimately deals their love a fatal wound.

Theme

The second half of the scene switches its focus from the theme of feuding and violence to the play's other key theme, love. Romeo woefully bemoans his plight as an unrequited, Petrarchan lover. The term *Petrarchan* comes from the poet, Petrarch, who wrote sonnets obsessively consumed with his unrequited love for Laura. Romeo's feelings of love have not been reciprocated by Rosaline, and this predicament causes him to dwell on his emotional torment.

Shakespeare chooses language that reflects youthful, idealized notions of romance. Romeo describes his state of mind through a series of oxymorons—setting contradictory words together—blending the joys of love with the emotional desolation of unrequited love: "O brawling love, O loving hate." That he can express such extreme emotions for a woman he barely knows demonstrates both his immaturity and his potential for deeper love.

Style & Language

Romeo's use of traditional, hackneyed poetry in the early stages of the play show him as a young, inexperienced lover who is more interested in the concept of being in love, than actually loving another human being. As the play progresses, Romeo's use of language shifts as he begins to speak in blank verse as well as rhyme. Through this development, his expressions sound more genuine rather than like a poem learned by rote. Shakespeare elevates Romeo's language as he elevates Romeo's love for Juliet.

Romeo's emotional turmoil also reflects the chaos of Verona, a city divided by the feud between the Montagues and the Capulets. Just as the city is embattled by the feud between the families, Romeo is embattled by his unrequited love for Rosaline. Romeo illustrates his idea of love as a battlefield by using military terms to describe the ways in which he has used his eyes and words of love in a combined attack to win the lady over, but without success: "She will not stay the siege of loving terms / Nor bide th' encounter of assailing eyes." Shakespeare repeatedly demonstrates how closely intertwined battles of love and hate can be. These conflicting images of love and violence ominously anticipate the play's conclusion when the deaths of Romeo and Juliet "win" the end of the feud.

Glossary

we'll not carry coals an old-fashioned saying, which meant to submit to insults.

colliers coal miners.

draw your neck out of collar Gregory puns on the word "draw" here, implying that Sampson will draw or slip his head out of a hangman's noose (collar).

maidenhead virginity.

I will bite my thumb at them, which is a disgrace to them if they bear it an Italian insult, a provocative, probably obscene gesture.

bills medieval weapons having a hook-shaped blade with a spike at the back, mounted on a long staff.

partisans broad-bladed weapons with a long shaft, used especially in the 16th century.

purple fountains jets of blood.

mistemper'd bad-tempered, angry; here, also referring to weapons which have been tempered, or made hard, in blood rather than water.

moved angry.

artificial night Romeo's behavior is unnatural (artificial).

true shrift confession.

love so gentle in his view love, often represented as Cupid, appears gentle.

in proof when actually experienced.

stay undergo.

posterity Rosaline's celibacy will prevent her passing on her beauty to her children or descendants.

forsworn promised not to love.

do I live dead Romeo regards Rosaline's decision to remain chaste as a form of living death.

ACT I
Scene 2

Summary

Paris, a relative of the prince, asks Capulet for his daughter Juliet's hand in marriage. Capulet is initially reluctant to give his consent because Juliet is so young. Finally, however, he agrees to the match if Paris can gain Juliet's consent.

Capulet invites Paris to a feast to be held that night. Capulet sends off the guest list with a servant, who is, unfortunately, illiterate and cannot read the names. He meets Romeo and Benvolio whom he asks for help. The guest list includes Rosaline, the object of Romeo's affections, so Romeo resolves to go to the feast despite the danger involved. Benvolio hopes that Romeo will see another lady there to help him forget about Rosaline. Romeo again denies that this could happen.

Commentary

Theme

Paris and Capulet's discussion of Juliet's age in the beginning of this scene continues another of the play's resounding themes: youth versus old age. In the world of the feud, the older generation's conflicts and bids for power control the destinies of their children without much apparent thought for their children's ultimate welfare. Thus the flaws in this patriarchal system make Romeo and Juliet's waywardness in love seem all the more innocent.

Capulet worries that Juliet, at 13, is too young to be married. He cautiously advises Paris: "Let two more summers wither in their pride / Ere we may think her ripe to be a bride." Shakespeare's emphasis on Juliet as a teenage girl poised between childhood and adulthood highlights that Juliet is a very young tragic heroine who is forced to mature extremely quickly during the course of the play.

Although Juliet's parents, like Romeo's, seem to look out for their child's best interests, Juliet's position is clearly subordinate to her father's political concerns. In the discussion of her marriage, Juliet is primarily a commodity. Paris wants her mainly because of her social status and beauty. Capulet may even be using her youth and innocence as "selling points" to Paris rather than expressing genuine fatherly concern for protecting her from the corruption of the big wide world. No sooner does he insist that Paris win Juliet's consent than he arranges the feast where Paris may woo her more easily.

Her father's half-hearted nod to gaining her consent is the last evidence of Juliet being empowered by her family. Hereafter, fate and her family control the marionette strings. Her actions (although not her words) are contrary to the powers that try to control her. Although her defiance doesn't become manifest until she refuses to marry Paris, this passage is both the twilight of her permissive independence and a harbinger of her defiant independence.

Character Insight

This scene presents Paris and Romeo as unwitting rivals for Juliet's hand. Paris is the model suitor—a well-to-do relative of the prince and notably courteous toward Capulet. He complies with social convention in his public proposal of marriage. Romeo, on the other hand, appears as a fanciful and fashionable young lover, with idealistic concepts of love. Romeo is reckless in his attitude towards love, quickly transferring his affections from Rosaline to Juliet, whereas Paris remains constant in his affection for Juliet. When Romeo falls in love with Juliet, he defies social conventions and woos her in secret.

A chance encounter with Capulet's illiterate servant later in the scene enables Romeo and Benvolio to find out about the feast. This chance meeting contributes to a sense of inevitability that Romeo and Juliet are destined to meet.

In his concluding speech, Romeo is only able to describe his feelings for Rosaline through figurative language that he has learned from poetry books. His borrowed images of love as a religious quest suggest that his idealism has separated him from reality; he is in love with an ideal, not a real person. Also borrowed second-hand from the sonnets are his images of "looking"—his declaration that his eyes cannot delude him only proves that he is the stereotypical lover blinded by love. This paradox builds dramatic suspense for Act I, Scene 5 when he falls in love at first sight with Juliet.

Glossary

suit the act of wooing; courtship.

well-apparell'd April clothed or adorned with images of new growth associated with the spring, such as leaves and blossom. Contrast with "limping winter."

sirrah a contemptuous term of address, here used to indicate the difference in social status between Capulet and his servant.

new infection to thy eye Benvolio continues to encourage Romeo to look for another love. Ironically, Romeo and Juliet fall in love at first sight.

plantain leaf the leaf was used to heal cuts and bruises. Romeo replies sarcastically that Benvolio's suggestion of a cure for Romeo's love melancholy would be as effective as applying a plantain leaf.

unattainted unprejudiced.

transparent heretics Romeo says that if he saw another woman more beautiful than Rosaline his tears would turn to fire and burn his eyes as "transparent heretics" for lying.

poised balanced, weighed.

crystal scales Romeo's eyes are like the pans on a set of crystal scales.

ACT I
Scene 3

Summary

Lady Capulet questions Juliet regarding her feelings about marriage and then informs Juliet of Paris' proposal. When her mother mentions that Paris will attend the feast that evening, Juliet reacts with dutiful reserve, whereas her nurse, recalling incidents from Juliet's childhood, volunteers a bawdier response.

Commentary

This scene introduces Juliet on stage and explores the theme of youth versus old age and the difference in attitudes between the Nurse, Lady Capulet, and Juliet towards love and marriage. The Nurse's uninhibited attitude towards sex is contrasted with Lady Capulet's reserved discussion of Juliet's proposed marriage to Paris.

Character Insight

The Nurse is a comic character who is a foil for Juliet, contrasting Juliet's youthful innocence with the Nurse's older, courser outlook on life. The Nurse's reminiscence about Juliet's being weaned and learning to walk also anticipates Juliet's move towards sexual maturity. For example, in her account of when Juliet fell over learning to walk, the Nurse recalls that her own husband noted bawdily: "Thou wilt fall backward when thou hast more wit." Such comments help depict Juliet as an adolescent on the threshold of womanhood, while reinforcing the idea that Juliet has been objectified as a marriage commodity since birth.

Juxtaposed with the Nurse's reflections on Juliet's childhood is Lady Capulet's discussion of the proposed match between Juliet and Paris. In her relationship with Juliet, Lady Capulet seems distant and cold, expecting Juliet's complete obedience in agreeing to the marriage. Juliet is clearly reluctant to agree to the arranged marriage as she says demurely: "It is an honor that I dreamt not of." Lady Capulet considers Juliet to be old enough for marriage: Besides, a marriage to Paris would bring increased social status and wealth for the Capulets, as Lady Capulet observes: "So shall you share all that he doth possess."

While Lady Capulet sees Paris as the chance to make a socially advantageous match for the family, rather than considering Juliet's feelings, the Nurse regards marriage as a purely physical relationship, almost a burden women simply must bear. She reinterprets Lady Capulet's line that marriage increases a woman's wealth and status as referring instead to the way in which marriage increases a woman through pregnancy. Thus, neither her mother nor her Nurse addresses the romantic concept of love that Juliet harbors. In fact, each identifies a distinct aspect of female oppression—social and physical.

Character Insight

Juliet's response to her mother's wish for her to agree to the marriage is clever and evasive: "I'll look to like, if looking liking move / But no more deep will I endart my eye." This answer indicates Juliet's emotional maturity because she has made up her own mind that she cannot marry someone whom she does not love, rejecting both her mother's and the Nurse's materialistic and sexual views of love. While she seems to acquiesce to tradition, her words suggest an awareness that there must be something better, beyond the concept of marriage that reinforces female social subordination.

Juliet's attitude anticipates her rebellion against her parents later in the play; as the gap between Juliet and her family widens. Juliet's view of love also points to the spiritual quality of her love for Romeo, which is not tainted by economic and sexual concerns. Because her concept of love transcends the temporal issues of family feuds, oppression of women, and generational differences, it is doomed to become the victim of those jealous forces.

Glossary

Lammas-tide a harvest festival formerly held in England on Aug. 1, when bread baked from the first crop of wheat was consecrated at Mass. The festival is used to symbolize fertility and plentitude, qualities which can be linked to Juliet as a young adolescent.

laid wormwood to my dug rubbed wormwood on my nipple: a method of weaning children. The Nurse's role when Juliet was a young child was to act as her wet-nurse and breast-feed Juliet.

tetchy touchy; irritable; peevish.

trow think.

by th'rood an oath: by Christ's cross.

broke her brow fell and cut her forehead.

by my holidame from the Anglo-Saxon for holiness, here used by the Nurse to mean "holy dame," that is, the Virgin Mary.

young cockerel's stone young rooster's testicle.

stinted stopped crying.

disposition inclination.

he's a man of wax he's perfect, without fault, like a wax figure.

endart shoot as a dart.

ACT I
Scene 4

Summary

Romeo, Benvolio, Mercutio, and others from the Montague household make their way to the Capulet feast. With their masks concealing their identity, they resolve to stay for just one dance.

Because Romeo continues to be lovesick for Rosaline, Mercutio teases him for being such a stereotypical hopeless lover. Mercutio then delivers his highly imaginative Queen Mab speech in which he describes how the fairy delivers dreams to humans as they sleep.

The scene concludes with Romeo's sense of foreboding at the forthcoming evening:

> my mind misgives
> Some consequence yet hanging in the stars
> Shall bitterly begin his fearful date
> With this night's revels.

Commentary

Character Insight

Mercutio acts in contrast to the lovestruck Romeo and the peaceful Benvolio—he is a witty and quick-tempered skeptic. Mercutio teases Romeo for his love melancholy by sarcastically using conventional images of Petrarchan infatuation to underscore Romeo's naive view of love. For example, when Romeo refuses to dance at the feast because his soul is overburdened with unrequited love, Mercutio mocks: "You are a lover, borrow Cupid's wings / And soar with them above a common bound." Mercutio is an anti-romantic; for him, love is a physical pursuit, which he emphasizes through his bawdy wordplay: "If love be rough with you, be rough with love / Prick love for pricking and you beat love down." Mercutio's repeated references to the sexual aspect of love casts Romeo's transcendent love for Juliet in a more spiritual light.

Mercutio treats the subject of dreams, like the subject of love, with witty skepticism, as he describes them both as "fantasy." Unlike Romeo, Mercutio does not believe that dreams can foretell future events. Instead, painting vivid pictures of the dreamscape people inhabit as they sleep, Mercutio suggests that the fairy Queen Mab brings dreams to humans as a result of men's worldly desires and anxieties. To him, lawyers dream of collecting fees and lovers dream of lusty encounters; the fairies merely grant carnal wishes as they gallop by. In juxtaposing lawyers and lovers, soldiers and the fairy entourage, his eloquent speech touches on a number of the play's opposing themes such as love and hate, fantasy and reality, idealism and cynicism.

It also gives insight into Mercutio's antagonistic and cynical nature: His description of the lovers is brief compared with the bloodthirsty image of the soldier who dreams of "cutting foreign throats." The beauty of the ladies' lips is quickly followed by the image of Mab blistering their lips with plague sores because the women had eaten too many sweets. Mercutio is down-to-earth, whereas Romeo continues to indulge in idealistic, lovelorn daydreaming. Indeed, his dream speech contains all the elements that will conspire to bring down Romeo and Juliet's starry-eyed dream of love to the depths of the tomb.

Style & Language

Romeo's final speech anticipates his meeting with Juliet and creates an atmosphere of impending doom, which undercuts the festivities. Instead of a date with a pretty girl on a starlit night, he intuits that he goes to a date with destiny. The heavy tone of this premonition is far more serious than the shallow melancholy Romeo has so far expressed. The cosmic imagery of "some consequence hanging in the stars" echoes the prologue in which Romeo and Juliet are presented as "star-cross'd" lovers, whose destinies are tragically interlinked.

Glossary

hoodwink'd blindfolded.

common bound ordinary limit, with a pun on "bound," as bound to leap about and to be confined.

a pitch falconry term used to describe the height from which a bird of prey swoops to seize its prey.

case mask.

quote note or observe.

Queen Mab a fairy queen who controls people's dreams.

agate stone a hard, semiprecious stone.

atomi creatures as small as atoms.

long spinners' legs the legs of the crane fly.

sweetmeats any sweet food or delicacy prepared with sugar or honey.

suit a petition at court which requires the influence of the courtier for it to be heard, for which he will receive financial reward.

benefice an endowed church office providing a living for a vicar, rector, etc.

ambuscados ambushes.

Spanish blades the best swords were made with Spanish steel.

vain fantasy misleading flights of imagination. This is how Mercutio perceives love.

misgives feels fear, doubt, or suspicion.

ACT I
Scene 5

Summary

Romeo and his fellow attendees arrive at the Capulet feast. The guests are greeted by Capulet, who reminisces with his cousin about how long it has been since they both took part in a masque. Romeo sees Juliet and falls in love with her instantly. Tybalt recognizes Romeo's voice and sends for his rapier to kill him. A violent outburst is prevented as Capulet insists on Tybalt's obedience, reminding him of Romeo's good character and the need to keep the peace.

Romeo and Juliet continue their exchanges and they kiss, but are interrupted by the Nurse, who sends Juliet to find her mother. In her absence, Romeo asks the Nurse who Juliet is and on discovering that she is a Capulet, realizes the grave consequences of their love. The feast draws to a close and Romeo leaves with Benvolio and the others. Juliet then discovers from the Nurse that Romeo is a Montague.

Commentary

The theme of youth versus old age is again evident in this scene through Capulet's interaction with his guests and relatives, particularly Tybalt. The reminiscence with his cousin about the masques they danced in as young men emphasizes his position within the play as an old man past his "dancing days."

Style & Language

When Romeo sees Juliet for the first time, he is struck by her beauty and breaks into a sonnet. The imagery Romeo uses to describe Juliet gives important insights into their relationship. Romeo initially describes Juliet as a source of light, like a star, against the darkness: "she doth teach the torches to burn bright! It seems she hangs upon the cheek of night." As the play progresses, a cloak of interwoven light and dark images is cast around the pair. The lovers are repeatedly associated with the dark, an association that points to the secret nature of their love because this is the time they are able to meet in safety. At the same time, the light that surrounds the lovers in each other's eyes grows brighter to the very end, when Juliet's beauty even illuminates the dark of the tomb. The association of both Romeo and Juliet with the stars also continually reminds the audience that their fate is "star-cross'd."

Romeo believes that he can now distinguish between the artificiality of his love for Rosaline and the genuine feelings Juliet inspires. Romeo acknowledges his love was blind, "Did my heart love till now? Forswear it, sight / For I ne'er saw true beauty till this night."

Romeo's use of religious imagery from this point on—as when he describes Juliet as a holy shrine—indicates a move towards a more spiritual consideration of love as he moves away from the inflated, overacted descriptions of his love for Rosaline.

Such ethereal moments of the expression of true love never last long within this feuding society. The threat of violence immediately interrupts the romantic atmosphere created by Romeo's sonnet when Tybalt recognizes Romeo's voice and wants to kill him then and there. Although forced to accept Capulet's decision as head of the family to allow Romeo to stay, Tybalt utters a threat that indicates that he will disregard Capulet's command, as he does in Act II, Scene 4, when he sends a challenge to Romeo. In presenting these complex social interactions in a public space, the play explores not only the conflict between the two feuding families but also the conflict within the families and across the generations. All the intertwined motivations become a snare for Romeo and Juliet's newfound love.

Theme

Romeo proceeds to woo Juliet with another sonnet which continues to use the religious imagery begun in the first sonnet to emphasize the wonder and spiritual purity of his love. Flirting with his pure approach, Juliet teases Romeo as a lover who kisses according to convention rather than from the heart, but the audience recognizes that he has already shed most of his pretenses. Romeo and Juliet are so enrapt completing the sonnet and gazing into each other's sparkling eyes that they forget to ask one another for names; instead, both discover from the Nurse the other's identity. In an instant, Juliet concisely expresses the connection between love and hate and marriage and death: "My only love sprung from my only hate." She also declares immediately that if she cannot marry Romeo, she would rather die: "If he be married. / My grave is like to be my wedding bed." The image of death as a bridegroom for Juliet is repeated throughout the play to maintain an atmosphere of impending tragedy.

Glossary

trencher a wooden board or platter on which to carve or serve meat.

marchpane marzipan, a confection of ground almonds, sugar, and egg white made into a paste and variously shaped and colored.

visor mask.

Pentecost a religious festival, the seventh Sunday after Easter.

antic face Romeo's face is still covered by his mask.

to fleer to laugh derisively (at); sneer or jeer (at).

portly dignified or well-mannered.

disparagement disrespect.

an ill-beseeming semblance an unfitting or inappropriate outward appearance or aspect.

set cock-a-hoop be boastful or conceited. Capulet is concerned that Tybalt's anger and lack of restraint will spoil the feast.

princox a coxcomb; fop. Capulet is keen to belittle Tybalt and force him to submit to his will as head of the household.

bitt'rest gall bitter feeling; rancor. Gall is another name for bile, one of the bodily humors (that is, bodily fluids thought to be responsible for one's health and disposition).

holy palmers' kiss a palmer is a pilgrim who carried a palm leaf to signify the making of a pilgrimage to the Holy Land. For Romeo, love is likened to a religious quest.

you kiss by th'book that is, according to convention.

marry an exclamation of surprise. "Marry" is a respelling of (the Virgin) "Mary."

the chinks plenty of cash.

fay faith; used in oaths as here.

prodigious both wonderful and portentous.

Act II, Prologue

Act II opens with a prologue in sonnet form that highlights two key points: how Romeo is affected by meeting Juliet and the difficulties the lovers will face as members of two opposed families.

The opening lines of the Prologue address the speed with which Romeo and Juliet have fallen in love, while poking fun at the way Romeo has abandoned his pursuit of Rosaline.

The Prologue does little to enhance the story and is often omitted when the play is performed. Many critics feel that a different author added the Prologue at some point after the play was originally written. Nonetheless, this introductory material serves to distinguish between Romeo's cold, miserable, unrequited love for Rosaline and his true, intensely mutual love with Juliet.

Unlike the first Prologue, this one speaks less of fate; rather, it helps to build suspense. "But passion lends them power, time means, to meet / Temp'ring extremities with extreme sweet." Romeo and Juliet forge onward in pursuit of their love—empowered to dare cross thresholds that have before been barriers.

Glossary

foe supposed that is, because Juliet is a Capulet.

complain lament as a lover.

she steal . . . hooks emphasizes the pleasures and dangers of Romeo and Juliet's love for each other. The love is a sweet bait or lure and the fearful hooks allude to Romeo's status as a Montague.

use are accustomed to.

tempering . . . extreme sweet mixing the difficulties facing Romeo and Juliet's relationship with love. Tempering refers to the process used to make steel, and here it is implied that Romeo and Juliet's love is strengthened by the obstacles they face as members of opposing families.

ACT II
Scene 1

Summary

This scene takes place outside the Capulet orchard. Romeo hopes to see Juliet again after falling in love with her at first sight during the Capulet masquerade ball. He leaps the orchard wall when he hears Mercutio and Benvolio approaching. His friends are unaware that Romeo has met and fallen in love with Juliet. Mercutio beckons to Romeo by teasing him about Rosaline's seductive beauty. Romeo continues to hide, and Benvolio persuades Mercutio to leave the scene, knowing Romeo's love of solitude.

Commentary

In this scene, Romeo begins a separation from his friends that continues throughout the play. His inability to reveal his love of a Capulet heightens his isolation. By leaping the wall surrounding the Capulet orchard, Romeo physically separates himself from Mercutio and Benvolio—a separation that reflects the distance he feels from society, his friends, and his family.

Romeo previously wallowed in a "prison, kept without food" (I.2.55) as his unrequited love for Rosaline withered from lack of reciprocation. Having joked at Romeo's Petrarchan miseries earlier in the play, Mercutio now adds a more cutting edge to his barbs. He calls to Romeo using physical and sexual innuendo to describe the female allure. To Mercutio, love is a conquest, a physical endeavor. Mercutio jests that Romeo will think of Rosaline as a medlar fruit, which was supposed to look like the female genitalia, and himself as a poperin pear shaped like the male genitalia.

Romeo's leap over the Capulet wall is symbolic of his flight to a spiritual conceptualization of love. He has moved beyond Mercutio's crude understanding of love—"quivering thigh, / And the demesnes that there adjacent lie"—to a less physical, more mystical perception of love.

Style & Language

Romeo describes Juliet in light images—conspicuously nonphysical descriptions. When he first sees Juliet, he says, "she doth teach the torches to burn bright." Romeo has often sought sanctuary in the dark, but the deepest shade has never satisfied him. Recall that he locked himself away in his room and shut the windows to create an "artificial night" while pining for Rosaline in Act I, Scene 1. Juliet transports him from the dark into the light, moving Romeo to a higher spiritual plane. Ironically, however, Romeo and Juliet's clandestine love can only flourish under the shelter of night.

Glossary

dull earth Romeo's description of himself.

conjure to summon a demon or spirit as by a magic spell. Mercutio attempts to raise or draw Romeo from his hiding place.

when King . . . lov'd the beggar maid a 16th-century ballad.

the ape is dead Romeo is described as a performing monkey who is playing dead and will not respond to Mercutio's conjuration.

demesnes a region or domain. Here Mercutio uses it to refer bawdily to the female genitalia.

to raise a spirit in his mistresses circle Mercutio puns on circle as both the magician's magic circle and the female genitalia.

consorted associated with.

medlars small, brown, apple-like fruit.

open-arse slang term for a medlar; "arse" is the buttocks.

poperin pear Mercutio compares the pear with the shape of the male genitals and puns on the name: pop-her-in.

truckle-bed a low bed on small wheels or casters, that can be rolled under another bed when not in use.

field-bed bed upon the ground.

ACT II
Scene 2

Summary

Romeo stands in the shadows beneath Juliet's bedroom window. Juliet appears on the balcony and thinking she's alone, reveals in a soliloquy her love for Romeo. She despairs over the feud between the two families and the problems the feud presents. Romeo listens and when Juliet calls on him to "doff" his name, he steps from the darkness saying, "call me but love."

After the two exchange expressions of devotion, the Nurse calls Juliet from the balcony. Juliet leaves, but returns momentarily. They agree to marry. Juliet promises to send a messenger the next day so that Romeo can tell her what wedding arrangements he has made. The scene concludes as day breaks and Romeo leaves to seek the advice of Friar Laurence.

Commentary

The scene contains some of the more recognizable and memorable passages in all of Shakespeare. Here, in the famous balcony scene, Romeo and Juliet reveal their love to each other, and at Juliet's suggestion, they plan to marry.

Shakespeare uses light and dark imagery in this scene to describe the blossoming of Romeo and Juliet's romance. As Romeo stands in the shadows, he looks to the balcony and compares Juliet to the sun. He then asks the sun to rise and kill the envious moon. Romeo had always compared Rosaline to the moon, and now, his love for Juliet has outshone the moon. Thus, as Romeo steps from the moonlit darkness into the light from Juliet's balcony, he has left behind his melodramatic woes and moved toward a more genuine, mature understanding of love.

The scene takes place at nighttime, illustrating the way Romeo and Juliet's love exists in a world quite distinct from the violence of the feud. Throughout the play, their love flourishes at night—an allusion to the forbidden nature of their relationship. As night ends and dawn breaks, the two are forced to part to avoid being discovered by the Capulet kinsmen. Romeo and Juliet fear that they might be exposed—that the artificial light of discovery might be shone upon them, thereby forcing their permanent separation.

Shakespeare describes the natural quality of their love by juxtaposing the balcony scene with Mercutio's lewd sexual jokes in the previous scene. Romeo returns to the religious imagery used between the lovers in their sonnets at the feast when he describes Juliet as, "a bright angel" and "dear saint." The recurring use of religious imagery emphasizes the purity of Romeo and Juliet's love—as distinguished from the Nurse and Mercutio's understanding of love that is constituted in the physical, sexual aspects.

Romeo begins to display signs of increasing maturity in this scene. His speeches are now in blank verse rather than the rhymed iambic pentameter evident in his earlier sonnets and couplets. Romeo is no longer the melancholy lover of Act I. Up to this point, Romeo has expressed his emotions in a traditional, colloquial style. His behavior has been notably antisocial—he preferred to submit to the misery of his own amorous failures.

Although Romeo has matured in the brief time since the beginning of the play, he remains somewhat immature when compared with Juliet—a pattern that recurs throughout their relationship. Although Juliet is only 13, she considers the world with striking maturity. As later acts reveal, her parents do not provide an emotionally rich and stable environment, possibly forcing Juliet to mature beyond her years.

Juliet shows the beginnings of increasing self-possession and confidence that ultimately lead her to seek her own fate rather than a destiny imposed upon her by her parents. Juliet introduces the idea of marriage to Romeo. She makes the practical arrangements for sending a messenger to Romeo the next day. Juliet stops Romeo from swearing his love on the moon as it is too "inconstant" and "variable." She stops him from using traditional, colloquial poetic forms in expressing his affection. She encourages him to be genuine and to invest himself in a less traditional, more spiritual concept of love.

Theme

Juliet's soliloquy examines another of the play's themes—the importance of words and names. Juliet compares Romeo to a rose and reasons that if a rose were given another name, it would still be a rose in its essence. If Romeo abandoned his family name, he would still be Romeo. Juliet calls into the night for Romeo to "refuse thy name" and in return, she will "no longer be a Capulet." Therein lies one of the great conflicts of the play—the protagonists' family names operate against their love. While their love blossoms in oblivion to any barriers, the people who affect their lives use their familial battles to impose separation upon the two young lovers.

Literary Device

Juliet's promise to Romeo to "follow thee my lord throughout the world" is full of dramatic irony and foreshadows the final scene of the play, when Juliet follows Romeo into death. Interruptions from the Nurse add to the atmosphere of intense urgency as the lovers frantically say good-bye. The heightened anticipation of their forthcoming marriage continues to build further tension and increase the pace of the play.

Glossary

her vestal livery chaste appearance or virginal dress.

sick and green pale and sickly. Green was the color associated with maids.

wherefore why?

doff discard.

enmity hatred; hostility.

prorogued delayed; postponed.

I am no pilot . . . should adventure for such merchandise Romeo describes himself as a merchant venturer, one who would make risky voyages to be with Juliet.

perjuries the breaking of promises.

Jove king of the Roman gods.

fond tender and affectionate; loving; sometimes, affectionate in a foolish or overly indulgent way.

strange reserved, aloof.

the god of my idolatry the object of my excessive devotion.

tassel-gentle from "tiercel," a falconry term for a male hawk, especially the male peregrine.

bondage is hoarse and may not speak aloud at home, Juliet is under her father's strict discipline and must whisper as though she is hoarse to avoid detection.

a wanton's bird that is, the pet of an undisciplined, spoiled child.

hap good luck or news.

ACT II
Scene 3

Summary

Romeo arrives at Friar Laurence's cell as day breaks. The Friar is collecting herbs and flowers while he postulates on their powers to medicate and to poison. Romeo tells him of his love for Juliet and asks the Friar to marry them later that day. The Friar is amazed and concerned at the speed with which Romeo has transferred his love from Rosaline to Juliet, but agrees to help the couple in the hope that the marriage might ease the discord between the two families.

Commentary

This scene introduces the Friar, a philosophical man who wishes to heal the rift between the families. His discourse on the healing and harming powers of plants will echo loudly later in the play. He will provide Juliet the sleeping potion that she drinks to avoid marrying Paris.

Theme

The dual nature within the Friar's plants suggests a coexistence of good and evil. The tension between good and evil is a constant force in this play—a strong undercurrent that conveys fate into the characters' lives. The Friar is a good example. His intentions are good; he wishes to end the feud in Verona. His plan, however, precipitates the tragic end to the play.

As the play progresses, the contentious coexistence of love and hate unfolds. Capulet loves his daughter, but treats her like his personal property. Romeo and Juliet's love exists in an atmosphere electrified by the darkness of the hatred between the families. The Friar's comment that "[t]he earth that's nature's mother is her tomb; / What is her burying grave that is her womb" harkens back to Capulet's statement about his daughter in Act I, Scene 2—"the earth has swallowed all my hopes but she."

The theme of nature destroying life in order to create life recurs frequently. While an undeniable certainty exists within this natural cycle, the Friar suggests that the deeply flawed human being imposes some degree of mutability on the entire process. Good and evil coexist in imperfect harmony. "Virtue itself turns vice, being misapplied; / And vice sometimes by action dignified."

The Friar is a religious idealist, a philosopher who understands the big picture while other characters in the play are too involved in their interrelationships to share his perspective. The Friar, like the herbs he collects, displays conflicting characteristics. He is a holy man, anxious to help the lovers in order to reconcile the Montagues and Capulets and bring peace to Verona. Yet his decision to marry Romeo and Juliet in a secret ceremony and deceive the Capulet family when Juliet takes the sleeping potion emphasizes the Friar's naive underestimation of the feud and the workings of fate—a failing that will prove deadly for Romeo and Juliet.

Romeo's relationship with the Friar again highlights the theme of youth versus old age, while underscoring Romeo's isolation from his friends and family. The Friar acts as a father figure to Romeo. The Friar is the only person to whom Romeo can confide the secret of his love for Juliet and his plans to marry. Romeo is typically impulsive and wants to be married that day whereas the Friar, using the formal language of rhyme, advises caution, reminding Romeo of the love he recently had for Rosaline and the speed with which he has abandoned that love.

Glossary

advance raise.

osier cage basket made from willow.

baleful harmful or poisonous.

virtues qualities.

mickle much or great.

residence the place in which a person or thing resides.

benedicite Latin for "bless you!"

distemperature a disordered condition, especially of the body or the mind.

holy physic spiritual remedy.

intercession prayers and petitions.

steads is of benefit to.

riddling puzzling or enigmatic.

shrift confession.

brine salt water; that is, tears.

by rote by memory alone, without understanding or thought.

rancour a continuing and bitter hate or ill will.

Act II
Scene 4

Summary

Now, the morning after the Capulet feast, Mercutio and Benvolio search for Romeo. Mercutio blames Romeo's absence on his love for the "pale, hard-hearted wench," Rosaline. Benvolio has discovered that Tybalt has sent Romeo a challenge to duel, and Mercutio is amused at the thought of an encounter between Romeo, the romantic, and Tybalt, the fashionable "Prince of Cats." Romeo then arrives and engages in a long series of linked puns and quibbles with Mercutio.

The Nurse arrives with her servant, Peter, looking for Romeo. Mercutio exasperates her with his quick, sharp mockery. Mercutio leaves with Benvolio, and Romeo tells the Nurse that Juliet should meet him at Friar Laurence's cell at 2 p.m. that afternoon to be married. The Nurse is to collect a rope ladder from Romeo so that he can climb to Juliet's window to celebrate their wedding night.

Commentary

Literary Device

Once melancholy and depressed by his passions, Romeo is now rejuvenated, buoyed by a renewed romantic energy after seeing Juliet at her balcony. Thoughts of his impending marriage have enlivened him to meet all of Mercutio's barbed, verbal challenges with equally gilded retorts. An air of excited anticipation energizes the atmosphere. Mercutio continues to ridicule Romeo as a Petrarchan lover for employing the popular love poetry of the sonnets. However, his speech is ironic because he still believes that Romeo is in love with Rosaline, and he never discovers Romeo's love for Juliet. These rapid, highly energized exchanges between the two friends reflect Romeo's own feelings of anticipation at his forthcoming wedding.

Mercutio, who has little patience for the emotional aspects of romantic pursuit, is delighted that Romeo has gotten over his lovesickness. Mercutio impishly engages in lewd wordplay and is preoccupied with the physical aspects of love. When Benvolio declares a truce in the talk between the two friends, Mercutio turns his verbal rapier on the Nurse, flustering her to distraction.

Theme

This mischievous repartee contrasts with the darkly ominous threats of Tybalt's challenge to duel Romeo. As in other parts of the play, vastly contrasting ideas coexist—love and hate; euphoria and despair; good and evil; levity and danger.

Character Insight

The news of Tybalt's challenge threatens to embroil Romeo in the violence of the family feud. While Romeo is well-liked in the community and has a peaceable reputation, Tybalt is a proud and vengeful foe. He is determined to confront Romeo despite Lord Capulet's opposition to continuing the feud. Although Capulet has forbidden any further violence, he remains the figurehead of the old conflict. "Fiery" Tybalt is Capulet's heir-apparent in carrying on the hostility since both men are quick-tempered and ready for a battle at a moment's notice. In contrast, Romeo is elated by his love for Juliet. His romantic idealism lightens his steps and carries him above these dark concerns.

The motive for Tybalt's quarrel with Romeo arguably stems from Tybalt's own masculine aggression rather than a sense of honor, thus emphasizing the trivial nature of the feud and Tybalt's isolation in maintaining the grudge.

The antagonism between Mercutio and Tybalt is intensely portrayed in this scene because both men are adversarial and quick-tempered. Mercutio scorns Tybalt's challenge and mocks him as someone more concerned with fashion than substance—a man who employs foreign styles of fencing and their terminology, which Mercutio regards as effeminate: "Ah, the immortal passado, the punto reverso, the hay!"

Style & Language

The sense of anticipation increases in this scene through repeated references to time. The Nurse's delay in finding Romeo amplifies an already intense sense of urgency. News that the wedding ceremony will take place at 2 p.m. illustrates the speed with which Romeo and Juliet meet and are to be married—in less than 24 hours.

Glossary

answer it accept it.

captain of compliments in dueling, one who has mastered all the rules and moves.

immortal punning on the moves as both famous and fatal.

passado a forward thrust.

the punto reverso a backhanded thrust.

the hay! term used to indicate that your opponent has been hit.

roe fish eggs.

conceive understand.

bow in the hams make a bow.

I'll cry a match I'll claim the victory.

natural fool; idiot.

bauble a jester's baton with an ornament at the end.

here's goodly gear a large clothes horse, refers to the appearance of the Nurse, who is also described in this scene as a sail. Romeo also continues Mercutio's series of bawdy puns in this scene, as gear refers to the reproductive organs.

ropery roguery.

flirt-gills loose women.

skains-mates cutthroat companions.

tackled stair rope ladder.

quit reward you for.

lay knife aboard lay claim to.

clout any piece of cloth, esp. one for cleaning.

Act II
Scene 5

Summary

Three hours after sending the Nurse for news from Romeo, Juliet waits impatiently for her return. The Nurse, knowing of Juliet's eagerness, deliberately teases the young bride-to-be by withholding the word of the upcoming wedding. Instead, the Nurse complains about her aches and pains. The Nurse finally relents when Juliet is almost hysterical with frustration and tells her that she is to marry Romeo that afternoon at Friar Laurence's cell. The Nurse then leaves to collect the rope ladder that Romeo will use to climb into Juliet's bedroom that night.

Commentary

The dizzying speed with which the lovers met, fell in love, and agree to marry is now contrasted with the way in which the hours appear to lengthen for Juliet as she waits for news. The emphasis on the passing of time evokes Juliet's parting lines to Romeo from the balcony in Act II, Scene 2, when he promised to send word to her the next day: "'Tis twenty years till then."

The scene echoes Romeo's discussions with the Friar because both Romeo and Juliet are desperately impatient to wed. Juliet's soliloquy and her subsequent exchanges with the Nurse show her youthful energy and enthusiasm in contrast with the Nurse, who is old, decrepit, and slow. Unlike her demeanor in other scenes, Juliet acts like a young teenage girl who has little patience for deferred gratification. Since the Nurse has been much more of a mother figure to Juliet than Juliet's biological mother, it follows that Juliet would feel free to act her age in the Nurse's presence.

The Nurse delivers Juliet news of her wedding—a message for a woman or young lady, not a 13-year-old girl. Maturity beckons Juliet with ominous, fateful overtones.

The Nurse's comic role increases the tension in this scene as she deliberately refuses to be hurried by Juliet in imparting her news. Juliet is forced to wait and coax the news from the Nurse, stifling her impatience when the Nurse continually changes the subject. The Nurse focuses on Romeo's physical attributes, describing his legs, feet, and hands in a speech that echoes Mercutio's description of Rosaline in Act II, Scene 1. Both the Nurse and Mercutio share a bawdy sense of humor and view love as a purely physical relationship.

The Nurse then comments knowingly on the pleasures that await Juliet on her wedding night with the pregnancy that will likely follow. This comment reflects the inverted life/death theme that runs throughout the play. Although Juliet will not live to give life, her death unifies her and Romeo in spirit and mends the feud—both forms of life-giving.

Glossary

nimble-pinion'd swift-winged.

bandy to toss or hit back and forth, as a ball.

feign to make a false show of; pretend.

jaunce trudge up and down.

coil commotion; turmoil.

drudge a person who does hard, menial, or tedious work.

Act II
Scene 6

Summary

Romeo and Friar Laurence wait for Juliet, and again the Friar warns Romeo about the hastiness of his decision to marry. Romeo agrees, but boldly challenges "love-devouring death" to destroy his euphoria. The friar then warns,

> These violent delights have violent ends
> And in their triumph die, like fire and powder,
> Which, as they kiss, consume

Juliet arrives and the Friar takes them into the church to be married.

Commentary

The wedding scene is notable for its brevity and pervasive atmosphere of impending doom. Images of happiness and marriage are repeatedly paired with images of violence and death. Romeo believes that not even death can counteract the pleasure he feels in marrying Juliet. This speech reflects both the impetuous and tragic nature of Romeo's love. Although he is unhesitating in his desire to be married to Juliet, Romeo's challenge to fate is prophetic and full of dramatic irony because it foreshadows his final speech in Act V, Scene 3, when death triumphs over both protagonists.

Style & Language

The explosive image in the Friar's "violent ends" speech recalls Montague's question in Act I, Scene 1, after the brawl: "Who set this ancient quarrel new abroach?" The term "abroach" was used to describe the way in which a barrel of gunpowder would be pierced to allow the contents to pour out and form a trail. The Friar's words are prophetic because he draws parallels between the destructive passion of Romeo and Juliet and the feud that will cause the violent deaths of Romeo, Juliet, Mercutio, Tybalt, and Paris.

Glossary

countervail to match or equal.

gossamers filmy cobwebs floating in the air or spread on bushes or grass.

vanity earthly pleasures or happiness.

blazen declare or celebrate.

Act III
Scene 1

Summary

During the heat of the day, Benvolio and Mercutio are loitering on the streets of Verona when Tybalt arrives looking for Romeo. Benvolio wishes to avoid a confrontation with the Capulets; however, Mercutio is deliberately provocative and tries to draw Tybalt into an argument so that they can fight.

Romeo appears and Tybalt insults him, hoping he will respond to the challenge, but Romeo refuses because he is now related to Tybalt through his marriage to Juliet. Mercutio, disgusted by Romeo's reluctance to fight, answers Tybalt's insults on Romeo's behalf. Tybalt and Mercutio draw their swords and fight. To stop the battle, Romeo steps between them and Tybalt stabs Mercutio under Romeo's arm. Mercutio's wound is fatal and he dies crying "A plague o' both your houses!" Blinded by rage over Mercutio's death, Romeo attacks Tybalt and kills him.

Romeo is forced to flee a mob of citizens as the Prince, the heads of the two households, and their wives appear at the scene. After Benvolio gives an account of what has happened, the Prince banishes Romeo from Verona under the penalty of death and orders Lords Montague and Capulet to pay a heavy fine.

Commentary

The hopeful tone of Act II changes dramatically at the beginning of Act III as Romeo becomes embroiled in the brutal conflict between the families. The searing heat, flaring tempers, and sudden violence of this scene contrast sharply with the romantic, peaceful previous night. The play reaches a dramatic crescendo as Romeo and Juliet's private world clashes with the public feud with tragic consequences. Mercutio's death is the catalyst for the tragic turn the play takes from this point onward.

True to character, the hot-headed Mercutio starts a quarrel the instant Tybalt requests a word with him, by responding, "make it a word and a blow." Tybalt at first ignores Mercutio's insults because, ironically again, he's saving his blade for Romeo.

Romeo, by contrast, is as passionate about love as Tybalt and Mercutio are about hostility. Romeo appears, cheerful and contented with having wed Juliet only hours before, and unaware that he's even been challenged to a duel. Until Mercutio dies, Romeo remains emotionally distinct from the other characters in the scene. Romeo walks atop his euphoric cloud buoyed by blissful thoughts of marriage to Juliet, peace, unity, and harmony. In response to Tybalt's attempts to initiate a fight, Romeo tells Tybalt that he loves "thee better than thou canst devise." Ironically, Romeo's refusal to duel with Tybalt brings about the very acceleration of violence he sought to prevent.

Character Insight

In Romeo's mind, he has shed his identity as a Montague and has become one with Juliet, his wife. Romeo's separation echoes the balcony scene where he said "Call me but love. . .Henceforth I never will be Romeo." However, Tybalt seeks revenge against Romeo because a Montague appeared at a Capulet ball. While Romeo no longer labels himself Montague, Tybalt still sees Romeo as standing on the wrong side of a clear line that divides the families.

Mercutio is disgusted by Romeo's abandonment of traditionally masculine aggression. Tybalt does not understand why Romeo will not respond to his dueling challenge—a traditional mechanism to assert and protect masculine nobility. Romeo's separation from these typical modes of interaction is both an abandonment of traditional masculinity and a departure from the temporal and divisive perspective of the feud. Romeo and Juliet's love embraces a transcendent, intensely unified concept of love. Their extraordinary love removes them from the animosity that drives the feud; however, that love is also flawed by Romeo acting out of anger rather than out of his love for Juliet.

Literary Device

Indeed, as soon as Mercutio confronts Tybalt on Romeo's behalf, Romeo's fall from his pinnacle of bliss seems destined. The hope that sprung from Romeo's marriage to Juliet is dashed in a few moments of swordplay. In a moment of profound irony, Romeo's attempt to stand between two combatants—his act benevolent of intervention—facilitates Tybalt's fatal thrust. Thus, Romeo's gesture of peace results in Mercutio's death and Romeo's becoming ensnared in the family conflict after all.

Mercutio's final speeches reflect a mixture of anger and disbelief that he has been fatally injured as a result of the "ancient grudge" between the Montagues and the Capulets; he repeatedly curses, "A plague o' both your houses." Even his characteristic wit turns bitter as Mercutio treats the subject of his own death with humorous wordplay: "Ask for me tomorrow and you shall find me a grave man." In the final irony of this scene, Mercutio never learns for what cause he was wounded. He believes he is wounded for a fight, not for a love. In shocked disbelief, he asks Romeo "Why the devil / came you between us? I was hurt under your arm."

Romeo blames himself for Mercutio's death because he placed his love for Juliet before consideration of his friend. Romeo thus attacks Tybalt to assuage his guilt. However, by doing so, he disregards any effect that his choice may have on Juliet. His action is impulsive and reckless. Romeo's rage overpowers his sensibility, and his fortunes are sealed. By attacking Tybalt in a blind fury, he has become one with fiery Tybalt; one with quick-tempered Mercutio, and one with the embittered patriarchs who originated the feud.

Theme

Tybalt's death brings Romeo a moment of clarity as he realizes that he is the helpless victim of fate: "O, I am fortune's fool!" he cries, struck deeply by a sense of anger, injustice, and futility. The speed with which Mercutio and Tybalt's deaths occur, together with Romeo's marriage and subsequent banishment, all contribute to a sense of inevitability—that a chain of events has been set in motion over which the protagonists have no control. Mercutio's dying curse upon the houses resonates as the voice of fate itself.

Glossary

abroad out and about.

by the operation of the second cup by the time the second cup of liquor has taken effect upon him.

addle muddled and, perhaps, rotten.

doublet a man's close-fitting jacket with or without sleeves, worn chiefly from the 14th to the 16th centuries.

tutor me from quarrelling teach me how to avoid getting into a quarrel.

simple feeble or foolish.

fiddlestick the bow for a fiddle. Mercutio puns on the word as he draws his rapier.

zounds an oath. The abbreviated form of the oath "By God's wounds."

bandying to give and take; to exchange (words) in an angry or argumentative manner.

sped done for.

ally relative, kinsman.

cousin loosely, any relative by blood or marriage.

aspir'd to rise high; to tower.

conduct guide.

amerce to punish by imposing a fine.

Act III
Scene 2

Summary

Juliet waits impatiently for night to fall so that she can celebrate her wedding night with Romeo. The Nurse arrives and in her grief, misleads Juliet into thinking that Romeo has been killed. When the Nurse eventually reveals that it is Tybalt who is dead, Juliet's fears are only slightly relieved. Upon hearing that Romeo has been banished, Juliet is overwhelmed by grief. The Nurse tells Juliet that Romeo is hiding at Friar Laurence's cell and Juliet sends the Nurse with a ring, bidding Romeo to come and "take his last farewell."

Commentary

Within the peaceful confines of the Capulet orchard, Juliet looks forward to the "amorous rites" of her marriage to Romeo. Juliet's impatience in anticipation of the nurse's arrival echoes her excited anticipation in Act II, Scene 5, when she had to wait for news of the wedding arrangements. A considerable sense of impending doom hangs in the atmosphere. Although she is unaware of the tragic news that awaits her, Juliet's soliloquy fantasizing about her wedding night embroiders tragic images into the fabric of her *epithalamion*, or wedding song.

Style & Language

Light and dark imagery again play important roles in creating mood, foreshadowing action, and giving fate a vehicle by which to visit itself upon the characters in the play. Juliet beckons the darkness because it has been a sanctuary for the couple, "if love be blind, / It best agrees with night." She and Romeo met under the cover of night; they agreed to marry as they were shrouded in darkness and were forced to part as dawn broke; they consummate their marriage at night; and they ultimately die together under the cover of night. Their affinity for the darkness illustrates their separation from the temporal, feuding world.

Although external light (the "garish sun") has become their enemy, the lovers have often provided light for each other. Juliet's eyes were like the stars in Act II, Scene 2, in Act I, Scene 5, she "doth teach the torches to burn bright!," and Juliet was Romeo's sun in the balcony scene. Here, Romeo brings "day in night." Juliet begs fate to "cut Romeo out in little stars" so that "all the world be in love with night." These stars represent both the timeless quality of the couple's love and their fate as "star-cross'd lovers" who will only truly be united in death.

Theme

The Nurse's report transforms Juliet from an anxious young bride into a bereft widow. Even when Juliet understands that Romeo is not dead, his banishment is equivalent to death in her eyes: "I'll to my wedding bed / And death, not Romeo, take my maidenhead." The association between Juliet and death as her bridegroom once again pairs the themes of love and death and emphasizes that her young life is constantly overshadowed by death.

Juliet feels conflicted because her love for Romeo clashes with her love and sense of duty to Tybalt, her cousin. Juliet expresses her conflicting emotions for Romeo using oxymoronic language: "Beautiful tyrant, fiend angelical."

The Nurse, on the other hand, expresses her feelings plainly. As part of the Capulet household, she grieves the loss of Tybalt as a family member. The Nurse praises Tybalt and blames Romeo for what has happened.

Character Insight

In fact, the Nurse's curse, "Shame come to Romeo" acts as a catalyst for Juliet, helping to clarify her feelings. Juliet's initial shock at Tybalt's death gives way to her intense feelings of love for Romeo and a notable transition in her character. Henceforth, Juliet's loyalty is firmly grounded in her love of Romeo and no longer predicated along family lines. She is now a wife first and a daughter, cousin, Capulet second.

The Nurse's inability to comprehend the intensity of Juliet's love for Romeo shows a significant development in her relationship with Juliet, who is emerging as a young woman with her own opinions and emotions. She no longer relies her Nurse for maternal guidance. The rift between the Nurse and Juliet foreshadows the final split in their relationship which occurs in Act III, Scene 5 when the Nurse betrays Juliet by advising her to forget Romeo and marry Paris.

Glossary

waggoner driver.

As Phaeton ... immediately Phaeton, the son of Apollo, was allowed to drive the chariot of the sun for a day. His reckless driving nearly set the earth on fire and Zeus, the king of the gods, struck him dead with a thunderbolt.

wink close and be unable to see.

civil night sober, serious night.

lose a winning match ... stainless maidenhoods that is, win Romeo by surrendering to him.

unmann'd untrained; also, as yet husbandless.

cords the rope ladder so that Romeo can climb up to Juliet's balcony.

death-darting eye of cockatrice a cockatrice is a fabulous serpent supposedly hatched from a cock's egg and having power to kill by a look.

bedaubed smeared or stained with blood.

divinest show excellent appearance.

all naught all wicked.

all dissemblers all liars.

aqua vitae alcoholic spirits.

tributary paying tribute.

modern commonplace.

Act III
Scene 3

Summary

Friar Laurence tells Romeo that the Prince has sentenced him to banishment rather than death. Romeo is distraught because he regards banishment as a form of living death when he cannot be with Juliet. The Friar tries to reason with Romeo, but young Romeo is inconsolable—"with his own tears made drunk." The Nurse arrives and tells Romeo of Juliet's grief. Hearing this, Romeo tries to take his own life, but is prevented by the Nurse. The Friar advises Romeo to go to Juliet that night as he had planned, and then before daybreak, flee to Mantua. The Friar promises to find a way to announce Romeo and Juliet's marriage publicly and thereby gain a pardon for Romeo to return safely.

Commentary

Character Insight

This scene parallels the previous scene where Juliet reacted to the news of Romeo's banishment with forceful emotion, yet controlled expressions of grief. In contrast, Romeo responds to his banishment with wailing hysteria and a failed suicide attempt. Their reactions show the clear differences between Romeo and Juliet's respective emotional maturity levels. Whereas grief-stricken Juliet lamented her fate, her marriage, and her life, Romeo falls to the floor grappling for a dagger with which to end his suffering. As when he attacked and killed Tybalt, he has little concern for the effect his actions will have on Juliet.

Romeo again rages against the tyranny his name has inflicted on his life. He angrily blames his name for the interfering with his romance with Juliet and wishes to cut from his body that part that houses his name. He distinguishes himself from his identity as a Montague by saying that it was "that name's cursed hand / Murdered her kinsman." The audience, however, readily observes that the effects of fate are amplified by Romeo's own impulsive behavior.

The Friar instantly links Romeo and Juliet's marriage with death when he says that Romeo is "wedded to calamity." The Friar's words echo Juliet's thoughts at the end of the previous scene when she says that Romeo's banishment will be a form of living death. Likewise, Romeo declares "Then banishéd' / Is death, misterm'd." Indeed, throughout the play, Romeo and Juliet are described as being wedded to death—these descriptions not only foreshadow the play's conclusion but also underscore fate as an omnipotent, controlling power that draws the characters inextricably toward their doom.

This scene is also driven by the conflict between the older and younger generations. The Friar chastises Romeo and reminds him of his good fortune that the Prince has commuted his sentence from death to a "gentler judgement" of exile. Although Romeo heretofore sought the wise counsel of Friar Laurence, a holy man of spiritual learning, now that Romeo's situation has grown critical, the Friar's advice is not as well received. The Friar's contemplative work is far removed from the blind passion and emotional torment that Romeo is experiencing. Romeo, in his agitated state, is unable to accept the calm, philosophical reasoning the Friar offers.

As in previous and subsequent scenes, the older generation's failure to comprehend the depth of Romeo and Juliet's passion isolates the lovers from sources of wisdom that might otherwise prevent their tragic fates.

Glossary

parts attractive qualities.

doom judgment.

world's exile Romeo feels exiled from the world.

validity value or worth.

state rank.

fond foolish.

Displant a town transplant a town; that is, do the near-impossible.

Taking the measure of an unmade grave Romeo is lying on the ground in despair.

simpleness foolishness.

conceal'd lady Juliet, Romeo's secret wife.

cancell'd love Romeo thinks that his killing Tybalt will render his marriage to Juliet null and void.

sack to plunder or loot.

rail'st complain.

usurer ... usest ... use indeed alliterative puns on "usury" and "use": Romeo is not putting his talents to their proper use.

form of wax not a real man, no more durable than a wax figure.

pouts upon treats with contempt.

blaze proclaim in public.

sojourn to live somewhere temporarily.

Act III
Scene 4

Summary

Late on Monday evening, Capulet and Paris discuss how Juliet's grief over Tybalt's death has prevented Paris from continuing his courtship of Juliet. Suddenly, as Paris prepares to leave, Capulet offers him Juliet's hand in marriage. He tells Paris that Juliet will obey his patriarchal wishes and marry Paris on Thursday. Paris eagerly agrees to the arrangements, and Lady Capulet is sent to convey the news to Juliet.

Commentary

The clash between parents and children, youth and old age, is further explored in this scene when Juliet's father suddenly decides that she should marry Paris as soon as possible. Whereas Friar Laurence tried to use the wisdom of his years to encourage the young, impetuous Romeo to have patience and bide his time until he could claim his bride, here Juliet's father makes rash plans for his daughter's future.

Literary
Device

Capulet's impulsive decision to hasten Juliet's wedding day precipitates the Friar's plot to have Juliet fake her own death to avoid the marriage. Capulet's repeated references to specific days and times create an oppressive sense of urgency as events rush towards their tragic conclusion. He reasons that since it is Monday night, Wednesday would be too soon due to Tybalt's death; therefore, Thursday would be an appropriate time for a wedding.

Capulet's confidence that Juliet will obey his will and consent to marry Paris contrasts sharply with his demeanor in Act I, Scene 2. At the masquerade ball, he told Paris he would agree to the match only if Juliet agreed. Now his assurances to Paris about his dutiful daughter's compliance are dramatically ironic because Juliet has already defied her father's authority, having married Romeo earlier that day. Indeed, the older generation is distinctly out of touch as Juliet is upstairs consummating her marriage to Romeo even as Capulet offers her hand to Paris.

Character Insight

Although Capulet's sudden change of heart appears arbitrary—he doesn't explain why the wedding must take place so quickly—the decision reflects his imperious and impetuous nature, which has undoubtedly kept the feud well-fueled. His language also suggests a shift from parental concern for his daughter's emotional maturity to consideration for her material comfort and social status.

Capulet, like his wife, is anxious to have his daughter marry successfully. In this scene, he conspicuously addresses Paris using a series of titles that indicate Paris' social superiority, "Sir Paris," "noble earl," and "My lord." Paris is a relative of the Prince, and as Capulet's son-in-law, would bring Capulet's family increased wealth and status. Capulet would never be able to understand, let alone agree to, a marriage for Juliet based solely on love.

Glossary

move persaude.

mew'd up a mew is a cage for molting hawks. Juliet has shut herself away to grieve.

desperate tender bold offer.

mark you me take notice of what I say; pay attention.

soft hush! Wait a moment!

Ha! ha! Capulet is reflecting on the plans he is making; he is not laughing.

ado fuss; trouble; excitement.

held him carelessly thought little of him, neglected his memory.

by and by soon.

Act III
Scene 5

Summary

At dawn on Tuesday morning, Romeo and Juliet make their final exchanges of love before Romeo leaves for Mantua. The lovers try to resist the coming day that heralds their separation by pretending that it is still night and that the bird they hear is the nightingale and not the lark, a morning bird. However, the ominous threat of the Prince's sentence of death finally forces the lovers to part.

Juliet's mother arrives and, believing that Juliet weeps for Tybalt rather than the departure of Romeo, tries to comfort Juliet with her plan to have Romeo poisoned. Lady Capulet then tells Juliet the happy news that she is to marry Paris on Thursday. Juliet is stunned and tells her mother that she cannot be married in such haste.

Her father enters expecting to find Juliet excited about the wedding he arranged on her behalf. When she expresses opposition, he becomes enraged and demands that Juliet obey his "decree" and prepare to be wed. The Nurse tries to defend Juliet, but to no avail. Capulet threatens to disown his daughter if she continues to oppose him. The scene concludes with the Nurse advising Juliet to obey her father, and Juliet resolves to seek the advice of Friar Laurence.

Commentary

Once again, the dawn divides Romeo and Juliet, this time, for good. As the sun's rays "lace the severing clouds," Juliet wishes the sound of the morning lark were actually the call of the nightingale. Juliet tries to deny the arrival of the coming day to prolong her time with Romeo. Their language is passionate and intense as Romeo agrees to stay and face his death. As in previous scenes, Romeo and Juliet's love flourishes in the dark, but daylight brings separation and ill fortune: Juliet says reluctantly, "window, let day in, and let life out."

Literary Device

As Romeo descends the balcony, Juliet experiences a frightening vision of Romeo "as one dead in the bottom of a tomb." This prophetic image will prove true in the final scene when Juliet awakens from her drug-induced slumber to find Romeo dead on the floor of the Capulet tomb. Once again, images of love and death intertwine, infecting the joy of their wedding night with the foreshadowing of their coming deaths.

Lady Capulet, unaware that Juliet grieves for Romeo's banishment rather than the death of Tybalt, tries to comfort her daughter with her plans to avenge Tybalt's death by poisoning Romeo. The speech is full of dramatic irony since Lady Capulet's hope of poisoning Romeo anticipates the method he chooses to take his own life in the final act of the play. Although Romeo drinks the poison by his own hand, it is the hatred, driven in part by Lady Capulet that gives him cause.

Character Insight

Far from a loving, maternal figure, Lady Capulet is cold and vengeful. She, like Tybalt, is prepared to continue the feud without regard to the authority of the Prince. Lady Capulet is brutally calculating— her venomous ire at Juliet's refusal to marry Paris leads her to say that she wishes "the fool were married to her grave." Once again the image of Juliet's grave as her wedding bed anticipates the lovers' tragic reunion in death. It is as if Lady Capulet, by her single-minded focus on the family feud, condemns her own daughter to her fate.

Juliet's interaction with both her mother and her father in this scene confirms the failure of parental love because their sole concern is with a socially acceptable marriage that will improve the wealth and status of the Capulet family rather than the happiness of their daughter.

When Capulet refused, in Act I, Scene 2, to consent to his daughter's marriage to Paris unless she also was willing, he seemed concerned for Juliet's welfare. Such parental concern altogether evaporates into authoritarian, patriarchal ranting as Capulet shouts epithets, calling Juliet "baggage" and "carrion" for refusing his order. Capulet now uses Juliet's youth to mock her reluctance to marry, calling her a crying child and whining puppet. Capulet has degraded his daughter to chattel— an item to be brokered for value. In his fury, Capulet threatens Juliet with violence and disinheritance if she continues to disobey him, "hang! Beg! Starve! Die in the streets! / For by my soul I'll ne'er acknowledge thee."

Character Insight

Capulet's sudden transformation from seemingly concerned parent to vengeful adversary illustrates his tendency toward impulsive, cruel, and reckless behavior. These tendencies may have contributed to the origination of the feud itself. He has shown such tendencies previously—he wanted to engage the Montagues in a sword fight using his long sword; he viciously denounced Paris for wishing to duel Romeo at the masquerade ball; and now he has turned on his only daughter with threats of disinheritance. He literally places her in a "nothing to lose" position and thereby encourages the defiance he resents so mightily.

While Juliet's parents react with extreme bitterness, Juliet handles herself with striking maturity. No longer the dutiful teenage daughter of the Capulets, she is a young woman, a bride, a wife. Her answers are skillfully truthful yet pragmatically deceptive. In response to her mother's desire to have Romeo killed, Juliet remarks that she "never shall be satisfied / With Romeo, till I behold him—dead." Juliet's mother interprets this as anger over Romeo killing Tybalt. However, in the Elizabethan vernacular, a man's death also means his sexual climax. Since Juliet has just ventured into the realm of physical love, she desires it again—both as a youthful desire for pleasure as well as a mature yearning for further spiritual contact with Romeo.

Character Insight

The Nurse, who has been more of a mother figure to Juliet than her biological mother, fails Juliet at this critical moment. To comfort Juliet in her desperate situation, the Nurse offers her an easy solution—marry Paris and forget the "dishclout" Romeo. This amoral recommendation betrays Juliet's trust and indicates the Nurse's inability to understand the passionate intensity and spiritual nature of Romeo and Juliet's love. After all, the Nurse regards love as a temporary, physical relationship, and she sees Juliet's marriage to Paris in entirely practical and economic terms.

The Nurse's failure to stand up for Juliet in the face of Capulet's onslaught is also understandable. She lacks Juliet's latitude to defy the Capulets. Although a loyal servant, the Nurse is not family and is keenly aware of her subordinated social position. She has been instrumental in facilitating Juliet's secret marriage and now seeks to cover the liabilities of her actions.

Each member of Juliet's primary family has abandoned her. Still a young person in need of an older person's support, she flees to the Friar as a source of aid and counsel. Juliet's isolation is nearly complete, and yet she is calm and resolute, as she determines to die rather than enter into a bigamous marriage with Paris: "If all else fail, myself have power to die."

Glossary

night's candles the stars.

Cynthia's brow the moon.

care desire.

hunt's-up morning song used to wake huntsmen and, more traditionally, a newly married bride.

runagate fugitive (runaway).

dram potion.

wrought arranged for.

mistress minion spoiled hussy.

hurdle a kind of frame or sled on which prisoners in England were drawn through the streets to execution.

hilding a low, contemptible person.

rate to scold severely; chide.

smatter to utter or gossip; an onomatopoeic word like "chatter."

demesnes the land around a mansion; lands of an estate.

puling fool whimpering child.

mammet doll or puppet.

challenge claim.

dishclout a cloth for washing dishes.

beshrew to curse: mainly in mild imprecations.

Act IV
Scene 1

Summary

On Tuesday morning, Paris tells Friar Laurence of his proposed marriage to Juliet—a wedding scheduled to take place in two days. The Friar expresses concern that the wedding has been arranged too quickly, and he offers various reasons to delay the ceremony. Paris believes that Capulet hastened the nuptials out of concern for Juliet's grief over Tybalt's death.

Juliet arrives at the Friar's cell and manages to cleverly sidestep Paris' compliments and references to their upcoming marriage. Paris then leaves, and Juliet begs the Friar for a solution to her tragic dilemma because she fears that death is her only option. The Friar offers Juliet a remedy—a sleeping potion that she is to take on Wednesday night, the evening before the wedding. The potion will render Juliet unconscious, and she will appear to be dead for 42 hours, during which time her body will rest in the family tomb. In the meantime, the Friar will let Romeo know of this plan. Juliet immediately agrees and leaves with the potion.

Commentary

This scene acts as a watershed—a defining moment—in the play's overall structure. In this scene, Juliet's decision to accept the Friar's potion demonstrates her commitment to defying her father's rule, asserting her independence, and accepting her resolution to die in order to be with Romeo.

Literary
Device

Juliet's composure in this scene is exceptional. She is surprised to find Paris at the Friar's cell—a development that contributes significantly to the dramatic tension in the scene. The tension in the cell is electric as Juliet and Paris engage in a rigid and formal exchange known as *stichomythia*—an exchange between characters in which their dialogue switches back and forth across alternating lines. Paris shows himself to be a proper and courteous suitor, while Juliet proves her nimble mind as she evades Paris's questions and compliments.

Paris, like Capulet, believes that marriage will cure Juliet's grief, which if left unsupervised, may result in extreme melancholy. Ironically, Juliet recently has made a series of mature, reasoned decisions, such as defying her family, marrying, and now, sacrificing her life for her forbidden love—all of which are contrary to Paris and Capulet's paternalistic view of her need for adult male guidance. Juliet's conversation with the Friar parallels Act III, Scene 3, because Juliet, like Romeo, now believes that only death can offer a solution to her dilemma: "Be not so long to speak. I long to die / If what thou speak'st speak not of remedy."

Literary Device

Juliet's describes her fears about pursuing the Friar's plan as she contemplates the horrors she is prepared to face rather than marry Paris. The gothic images foreshadow the play's final scene in the Capulet tomb. She prepares to take the potion and exclaims, "And bid me go into a new-made grave / And hide me with a dead man in his shroud." Although these images suggest the wild fears of a spirited young teenager, they also highlight her bravery and the depth of her love for her husband.

Character Insight

The Friar's willingness to help Juliet reflects his concern for his own role in the unfolding events. He has performed an illicit marriage and must now strive to prevent being implicated in the bigamous marriage between Juliet and Paris. The Friar has exposed himself to substantial personal liability, but he faces many opportunities to absolve himself of any involvement. The Friar is a peace-loving yet powerless character whose efforts to promote good are as subject to the whims of fate as anyone else's in the play.

Theme

The plan Friar Laurence concocts to place Juliet in a deathlike state so that she may emerge from the tomb to be reunited with her husband appears both farfetched and morbidly weird. In the context of the play, however, the plan manifests themes previously and repeatedly intertwined—love, marriage, life, and death. By placing Juliet into a suspended state, the Friar is reversing the traditional birth/death paradigm—he is creating death in order to draw out life. This theme echoes his words from Act II, Scene 3, "The earth that's nature's mother is her tomb. / What is her burying grave, that is her womb" (lines 9–10).

Through the Friar's plan, the cycle of life and death is reversed; Juliet must appear to die in order to share her life with her husband. Romeo and Juliet's love has transcended the hollow concerns of the other mortal players. Now in order to be united, Romeo and Juliet must rise above the troublesome, temporal world in which mortal players squander their lives in fighting and feuding rather than in living and loving.

The Friar uses his knowledge of flowers and herbs to conceive Juliet's remedial concoction. In Act II, Scene 3, the Friar describes the dual qualities of the flower that is capable of healing yet has the power to act as a poison. The drug the Friar offers Juliet is compounded of opposites and will give Juliet the appearance of death so that she can regain her life and her love. The Friar's plan serves as the mechanism of hope for Juliet, but due to the influence of fate, becomes the vehicle of the tragedy itself.

The Friar's plan to fake Juliet's death using a sleeping drug would have been accepted by Shakespeare's audience, because medical knowledge was extremely limited in the 16th century. Up to the mid-19th century, physicians often were unable to distinguish between deep comas and death, making real the possibility that someone could be buried alive. When her nurse discovers Juliet, the family accepts that she is dead simply from her appearance, without having the fact confirmed by a physician.

Glossary

nothing slow to slack his haste by no means reluctant if I should slow him down in his haste.

uneven is the course the decision is arbitrary and one-sided.

society companionship.

pensive sad; melancholy.

shield forbid.

prorogue postpone; delay.

extremes severe difficulties.

cop'st is willing to face or encounter.

charnel house a building or place where corpses or bones are deposited.

reeky emitting a strong, unpleasant smell.

chapless without the lower jaw.

humour fluid.

surcease cease; stop.

wanny pale.

supple government muscular movement.

stark stiff or rigid, as a corpse.

drift intention.

toy triviality.

Act IV
Scene 2

Summary

Juliet returns to the Capulet house to find wedding preparations well underway. She tells her father that she will abide by his wishes and agree to marry Paris. Lord Capulet is so overjoyed at the news that he decides to move the wedding from Thursday to Wednesday. Lady Capulet protests, saying that such quick notice doesn't allow enough time to prepare, but the euphoric Lord Capulet ignores her. Juliet is now to be married the following morning.

Commentary

Here, fate twists Juliet's fortunes once again. Capulet, in his impulsive zeal, complicates the Friar's plan by moving the wedding forward a full day. Juliet must take the potion that night and lapse into a suspended state 24 hours sooner than the Friar had anticipated. This development reduces the amount of time the Friar will have to notify Romeo in Mantua.

Juliet has acquiesced to Capulet's reckless whims and appears compliant—even excited to an extent. This enthusiasm, however feigned, seems to heighten her father's zeal even further. Juliet shows great composure in facing her father, even though she knows that his plans and her arrangements are so different. Juliet's enthusiasm is, however, at least somewhat genuine since the mechanism by which she intends to resolve her personal crisis is already in motion.

**Character
Insight**

Capulet, of course, misinterprets Juliet's apparent good cheer, believing that Friar Laurence has persuaded Juliet to marry Paris. Capulet is characteristically impulsive, rash, and unpredictable. His blind enthusiasm leads him to insist that his entire family and staff work through the night to make adequate preparations for the hastened ceremony. In this scene, he shows a greater disrespect for his wife than in previous scenes. His blathering authoritarianism reaches new levels as he again insults Juliet, accusing her of "peevish, self-willed harlotry." He completely dominates his wife, disregarding her desire to delay the wedding and ordering her to Juliet's room to help the Nurse.

Character Insight

The comparison between Juliet and her mother is noteworthy. Whereas Lady Capulet cannot exercise any control in her life and receives no respect from her husband, Juliet has taken control of her life and tries to exert some influence over her situation. She has become self-possessed to the extent that she can command her own fate; however, when society eliminates her options, she is left with the only thing she can control—her death.

Style & Language

Juliet displays remarkable powers of duplicity as she describes her meeting with Paris at the Friar's cell. She tells her father that she gave him, "what becomed love I might / Not stepping o'er the bounds of modesty." To Capulet, the statement confirms Juliet's total compliance with his wishes. Clearly, however, as Romeo's wife, Juliet's devotion to Romeo is absolute.

Character Insight

Juliet's duplicity goes beyond her skillful use of language. She partakes willingly in the wedding preparation; however, amid all the frenzy, Juliet prepares for her presumed death. She has emotionally removed herself from her surroundings. Her trust rests in the Friar and her love in Romeo. The Capulet household is alive with activity on her behalf— for an occasion she neither desires nor intends to attend. The people around her have betrayed her, and the wedding preparations manifest that betrayal.

Glossary

none ill no bad ones.

I'll try . . . fingers from the saying that only bad cooks will not be able to lick their own fingers; that is, the servants will see if they are willing to test their own cooking.

unfurnish'd unprepared, without supplies.

forsooth yes indeed.

harlotry willful behavior or hussy. Capulet regards his daughter with contempt.

gadding wandering about in an idle or restless way.

enjoined ordered.

becomed befitting; becoming.

bound obliged or indebted.

closet a small room or cupboard for clothes.

provision food and other supplies.

huswife a housewife.

Act IV
Scene 3

Summary

Juliet and her nurse make the final preparations for the wedding that is to take place the following morning. Lady Capulet offers her assistance, but Juliet asks to be left to her prayers and sends the Nurse and her mother away. Juliet then reflects on the Friar's plan. She wonders if the Friar has given her actual poison to cover his role in marrying a Capulet and a Montague. She decides she must trust the Friar. However if the potion fails to work, she resolves to die rather than marry Paris. To that end, she places a dagger by her bedside. Juliet's imagination runs wild as she imagines the horrors she will face if the plan does not work and she awakens alone in the tomb. Only when she imagines Tybalt's ghost moving toward Romeo to avenge itself does she muster the courage to take the potion and intercept Tybalt:

> O look, methinks I see my cousin's ghost
> Seeking out Romeo that did spit his body
> Upon a rapier's point! Stay, Tybalt, stay!

Commentary

Juliet asserts her independence in this scene by asking her betrayers, the Nurse and Lady Capulet, to leave her alone. By this action, she both physically separates herself from her family and proactively takes a step toward the fruition of her plan to be with Romeo. This direct request marks a turning point for Juliet. Previously, she often reacted to her surroundings rather than making her own decisions. For example, she waited for instruction from Romeo as to when they would wed; she allowed her father to order a marriage to someone else; and she depended on the Friar to provide her with a plan to avoid a union with Paris.

As the play has progressed, however, she has grown more mature and independent. She now steps forward to confront her greatest fears and reach toward her ultimate goal—to be with Romeo.

When Juliet is left alone, she is struck by the horror of her situation. She imagines the gruesome, grisly, nightmarish horrors one would expect of a 13-year-old facing her own mortality: being buried alive in the airless tomb and facing Tybalt's corpse "festering in his shroud." At that moment, she is tempted to call for her nurse. However, at the instant of her greatest fear, Juliet realizes that she must act independently. She displays mature courage and determination as she prepares to take the final step in her defiance of both her parents and fate itself. Juliet accepts that she must now trust the Friar's potion, and if the plan fails, be prepared to take her own life with the dagger at her bedside.

Once again, the play draws upon the themes of birth and death to emphasize the way in which Juliet must die and be placed in the tomb in order to be reborn to begin her new life with Romeo. She is resolute in her decisions. Her maturity has blossomed. She is no longer a young teenager; she is a woman and a wife who commands her own fortune. To this end, she places a dagger by her side—a resonant statement of her independence.

Glossary

orisons prayers.

state circumstances.

cross unfavorable.

culled picked out; selected.

behoveful necessary or required.

faint cold fear fear causing a chilling faintness.

subtly hath ministered cunningly has administered.

tried proved.

conceit thought.

receptacle repository or sepulcher.

shrieks like mandrakes   a mandrake is a poisonous plant whose root was thought to have magic powers because of its fancied resemblance to the human body. It was believed that the mandrake would shriek as it was pulled out of the ground, and to hear a mandrake's shriek was thought to bring death or madness.

environ'd with   surrounded by.

rage   insanity, madness.

Act IV
Scene 4

Summary

The time is 3 a.m., and Lord Capulet has not been to bed. The Capulet household has been alive throughout the night with frenetic wedding preparation activities. The day begins to break, and Capulet hears music signaling that Paris is approaching the house. He orders the Nurse to awaken Juliet.

Commentary

Literary Device

The Capulet house bustles with activity as the family feverishly prepares for the wedding ceremony. Banter with the servants is frenetic and excited. The atmosphere is electrified with the joyful expectation of the upcoming marriage. The commotion on the lower floors provides a striking contrast with the scene upstairs, where the bride lies in bed, apparently dead. Capulet's final line is ironic when he notes the arrival of Paris, "make haste! The bridegroom is come already."

Capulet is unaware that Juliet is already a bride and that her bridegroom is Romeo, not Paris. The appearance of the bridegroom also foreshadows Capulet's speech of lamentation in the next scene, when he describes death as a rival suitor for Juliet.

Glossary

pastry place where pastry is made.

curfew bell the bell used especially in the medieval and renaissance periods, which rang in the morning and evening to signal curfew.

cot-quean a man who usurped the place of the housewife. The Nurse teases Capulet for the pride and concern he takes in household affairs.

lesser cause that is, a woman, an amorous liaison.

you have been a mouse-hunt in your time you have chased after women in your youth. "Mouse" was an amorous term for a woman and here suggests the image of a cat prowling after a mouse.

jealous hood jealous wife. Caplet is humorously responding to his wife's remarks about his past.

loggerhead a stupid fellow; blockhead. Capulet puns on the second servant's ability to find logs for the fire.

Act IV
Scene 5

Summary

The scene opens early on Wednesday morning. The Nurse enters Juliet's room and discovers her seemingly lifeless body on the bed. The Nurse tries to wake her, but believing her to be dead, cries out to the family in desperation. The Capulets, Friar Laurence, and Paris enter the room in response to the Nurse's cries. They dramatically mourn Juliet's loss while the Friar maintains his deception by offering words of support about Divine Will, comforting the family by expressing the belief that Juliet is in heaven. He then arranges for Juliet's body to be taken to the family vault. Capulet orders that the wedding preparations be changed to funeral preparations. The scene concludes with a comic interlude between the wedding musicians and Peter, a Capulet servant, as they engage in bawdy wordplay.

Commentary

The Nurse opens this scene by bantering humorously—almost giddy in her hope and good humor as she speaks with brassy references to Juliet's wedding night. The Nurse anticipates that Juliet will get little sleep that night. The viewer knows, however, that the euphoria will be short-lived and that unspeakable sorrow awaits the Nurse. In the Capulet household, moods tend to change quickly. When the Nurse discovers Juliet's body, the tone of the scene immediately changes from excited anticipation to shocked sorrow.

Style & Language

Romeo and Juliet again are ensnared in the love/death/marriage matrix that has defined and described their relationship from the beginning. Lady Capulet's chilling words echo loudly here, "I would the fool were married to her grave" (III.v.141). Capulet, who earlier referred to his daughter as carrion, speaks his most eloquent lines in the play, "Death lies on her like untimely frost / Upon the sweetest flower of all the field." Recall Act I, Scene 2, when Capulet says "the earth hath swallowed all my hopes but she." These passages blend the Friar's concept of nature as a cyclical force taking life to give life.

Style & Language

Capulet bemoans the loss of his last hope; however, in a macabre mix of sex and death, he describes Juliet's death as a sexual experience, emphasizing the Elizabethan translation of death as sexual ecstasy. He tells Paris that death has taken Juliet's virginity: "There she lies / Flower as she was / deflowered by him." This passage echoes Juliet's woeful proclamation in Act III, Scene 2 "I'll to my bed; / And death, not Romeo, take my maidenhead!" (III.ii.137). Capulet continues saying "Death is my son-in-law." These images mournfully anticipate the consummation of Romeo and Juliet's deaths in the final act of the play.

Glossary

pennyworths small portions.

aqua vitae alcoholic spirits.

settled has stopped flowing.

deflowered by him having lost her virginity to him.

confusion's . . . confusions the solution is not to be found in this uncontrollable grief.

promotion advancement in rank.

she should be advanced that is, through the socially advantageous marriage to Paris.

in this love in your concern for her material and earthly well-being.

rosemary evergreen herb which was used as a symbol of remembrance.

ordained festival prepared for the wedding festivities.

lour scowl or frown upon.

pitiful case pitiful state of affairs.

merry dump here an oxymoron: a sad tune or song.

gleek a gesture of contempt or a rebuke.

pate the head, esp. the top of the head.

carry no crotchets put up with none of your notions or whims.

catling a small lute or fiddle string made out of cat gut.

prates talks much and foolishly; chatters.

rebeck a three stringed fiddle.

tarry for wait for.

Act V
Scene 1

Summary

In Mantua, Romeo mistakenly believes that his dreams portend good news because he dreamed that Juliet found him dead but revived him with her kisses. Romeo's servant, Balthasar, then reports to Romeo that Juliet has died. Romeo, controlling his grief, makes plans to return to Verona. He offers a poor apothecary a large amount of money to sell him poison illegally. The poison will enable Romeo to be reunited with Juliet in death.

Commentary

Although the audience might expect to find Romeo in Mantua wallowing in the depths of despair over his banishment, he is actually in very good humor. He has dreamed that he died and Juliet's kisses breathed life back into his body. But, as Mercutio says in Act I, Scene 4, "Dreamers often lie." Romeo's soliloquy is full of dramatic irony because the dream anticipates the play's final scene when Juliet awakes in the tomb to find Romeo dead and tries to kiss the poison from his lips.

Tragedy is imminent when Balthasar arrives wearing boots—a harbinger of doom in classical theater. Balthasar gently delivers to Romeo news that Juliet's "body sleeps." Because the Friar's message did not reach Romeo in Mantua, Romeo's good mood shatters instantly.

As fate again mischievously meddles in Romeo's life, his melodramatic idealism gives way to defiant anger, "I defy you stars!" Romeo rages against the malevolent influence of fate—a driving force in the play from the outset. Previously, Romeo lamented being "fortune's fool." Now, he acts out of frustration, anger, and bold defiance.

This moment of defiance marks a change in Romeo's character. Henceforth, he is angry, cynical, and emboldened to defy his fate. His anger and frustration drive him to try to take command over his own life—he decides that if he cannot be with Juliet in life, he will join her in death. His resolve to die echoes Juliet's expression that her last resort is her sanctuary—they have the power to die.

To this end, Romeo visits an impoverished apothecary. The apothecary's dusty, tomb-like shop is a museum of deathly horrors filled with the bodies of dead animals, "skins," "bladders," and "old cakes of roses." The apothecary wears tattered clothes; his face is hung with "overwhelming brows," and "[s]harp misery ha[s] worn him to his bones." This cadaverous apothecary, a personification of death, brokers deathly poison to Romeo.

Romeo wants a poison that will steal life "violently as hasty powder fired." This phrase recalls the Friar's admonition to Romeo that violent loves die "like fire and powder, / Which as they kiss, consume." (II.6.9–11). Haste drives one misfortune to collide with another throughout the play—each event teasing the reader with a morsel of hope, then lurching the action forward toward the tragic conclusion.

Romeo's hasty reaction to Mercutio's death causes his banishment from Mantua; Capulet's rash decision to move up the wedding day precipitates Romeo missing the message from the Friar; and later, Romeo's haste to consume the poison causes him to die just prior to Juliet's awakening. Haste throughout the play acts as a vehicle for fate to draw characters through a series of unfortunate coincidences that form the intricately intertwined plot of the tragedy itself.

Glossary

presage predict; forecast.

my bosom's lord love.

unaccustomed spirit unusually high spirits.

lifts me above the ground with cheerful thoughts Romeo is almost walking on air.

love's shadows dreams; visions.

post-horses horses kept at a post house, or inn, for couriers and post chaises or for hire to travelers.

weeds garments; clothing.

overwhelming overhanging.

culling of simples gathering herbs.

a beggarly account of empty boxes empty boxes of little worth.

remnants of packthread remains of strong, thick thread or twine for tying bundles, packages, and so on.

old cakes of roses dried rose leaves pressed into cakes.

penury extreme poverty.

caitiff wretched.

soon-speeding gear fast-acting.

utters sells.

cordial an invigorating medicine that stimulates the heart.

Act V
Scene 2

Summary

Friar Laurence discovers that Friar John, the messenger he sent to Mantua with a letter to Romeo explaining that Juliet is alive, has been quarantined because of an outbreak of the plague and prevented from leaving Verona. Friar Laurence then hurries to the Capulet tomb because it is nearly time for Juliet to wake.

Commentary

Fate has once again altered the course of events in the play. In this instance, fate thwarts the Friar's plan by delaying his letter. The Friar cries, "Unhappy fortune!" echoing Romeo's earlier cry that he became "fortune's fool."

The scene is driven by an overwhelming sense of desperation as the Friar returns to the Capulet tomb to liberate Juliet. The audience may recall the Friar's words from Act II, Scene 3, that the earth is nature's mother and that her "burying grave . . . is her womb." The Friar's desperate attempt to physically extricate Juliet from the womb-like tomb casts him in the role of symbolic midwife, who must deliver Juliet from the bowels of death. Now the philosophical Friar, more at home with ideas, must take action so that his entire plan does not decay into an abortive attempt to defy fate.

Glossary

barefoot brother another friar.

to associate me to accompany me.

searchers of the town health officers whose duty it was to view dead bodies and report on the cause of death.

nice trivial.

charge important matters.

dear import of serious concern.

crow a crowbar.

Act V
Scene 3

Summary

Paris arrives at the Capulet tomb to lay flowers in Juliet's memory. His page warns him that someone is approaching, and they hide in the bushes outside the tomb. Romeo appears with Balthasar and breaks into the tomb on the pretext of seeing Juliet one last time. Balthasar, apprehensive about what Romeo is going to do and fearful of Romeo's wild looks, also hides himself outside the tomb. Paris, believing that Romeo has come to desecrate the bodies in the tomb, confronts Romeo. Romeo tries to warn Paris off, but Paris challenges Romeo and they fight. Paris is wounded and dies. Just before he dies, he begs Romeo to place him in the tomb next to Juliet. Romeo is filled with compassion and grants his wish. Paris' page, who has watched the fight, goes to call the night watchman.

Romeo is dazzled by Juliet's beauty even in death. Without hesitation, he kisses her, drinks the poison, and dies at her side. A moment later, the Friar arrives and discovers the dead bodies of Romeo and Paris. Juliet then wakens from her death-like sleep and looks for Romeo, saying, "Where is my Romeo?" Upon seeing the bodies of Romeo and Paris, she resolves to remain in the tomb.

The Friar tries in desperation to convince Juliet to leave as the night watchman approaches, but Juliet refuses. The Friar flees, and Juliet is alone with Romeo and Paris dead at her side. She tries to drink poison from Romeo's vial. Finding it empty, she tries to kiss some poison from his lips. Hearing the night watchman approach, Juliet fatally stabs herself with Romeo's dagger.

The night watchman and the Prince arrive shortly, accompanied by the Capulets and Lord Montague. Lady Montague has died of grief at Romeo's banishment. The Friar faithfully recounts the events of the past week and offers his life in atonement. The Prince acknowledges the Friar's benevolent intent and instead lays the blame for the deaths squarely on Montague and Capulet for their longstanding quarrel. The Prince also blames himself for his leniency and fines Montague and

Capulet severely. The two families are finally reconciled as the Prince ends the play by saying, "For never was a story of more woe / Than this of Juliet and her Romeo."

Commentary

The final scene of the play brings both the transcendent reunion of Romeo and Juliet and the reconciliation of the feuding families. The family tomb becomes a symbol of both birth and death. It is, on the one hand, the womb from which Juliet should emerge alive—and hope be born anew. However, the tomb is also a dark and fateful vortex that consumes life, light, and hope. Romeo pledges in Act V, Scene 1, that he will defy fate and lie with Juliet that night. In his final act, he falls by her side and lies with her in perpetuity.

As Romeo charges into the tomb, a "detestable maw," he sheds much societal pretense that previously influenced his behavior. His plans are "savage-wild," "[m]ore fierce than empty tigers or the roaring sea," and he vows to tear anyone who attempts to detract him "joint by joint" and to "strew this hungry churchyard with thy limbs." Romeo has separated himself from his family, from the feud, from Verona, and now from his humanity.

This last scene, appropriately, takes place in the dark of night. Heretofore, Romeo and Juliet's relationship flourished at night, and each provided the other with light. In his final speech, Romeo once again uses light and dark imagery to describe Juliet as she acts as a source of light in the darkness of the tomb. "her beauty makes / This vault a feasting presence full of light." Such images simultaneously make the audience all the more aware of how close the lovers come to finding joy—making their end in darkness all the more tragic. However, these images also suggest a spiritual light that may surround a wedding feast for the couple beyond death.

Romeo is struck by the way Juliet's beauty appears to defy death—she still looks alive: "Why art thou yet so fair? Shall I believe / That unsubstantial Death is so amorous?" he asks bitterly, believing that death preserves her to be death's own lover. The dramatic tension is amplified by the audience's awareness that Romeo is seeing the physical signs of Juliet's recovery from drug-induced sleep. In an example of bleak irony, his attraction to her even in death emboldens him to press onward with his own suicide just as she is about to awaken.

Lady Capulet's curse on Juliet echoes loudly: "I would the fool were married to her grave," as does Paris' description of the tomb as a "bridal bed." Once again, the themes of love, sex, and death become inextricably intertwined ensnaring the characters in an intricate web. Reunion in this scene is not only spiritual, but also sexual. Shakespeare again draws on the Elizabethan meaning of death as sexual climax. Romeo drinks poison from the round vial—an allusion to female sexuality. Juliet stabs herself with Romeo's dagger, a phallic image symbolizing the reconsummation of their marriage. Thus as they die in pursuit of spiritual unification, they symbolically reconsummate their marriage, leaving their bodies as monuments to the depth of their love as well as signs of the tragic waste that is the feud's legacy.

Paris' challenge to Romeo at the tomb parallels Tybalt's challenge in Act III, Scene 1. In both instances, Romeo resists the invitation to fight, but fate conspires to leave him no choice. Romeo is reluctant to kill Paris, because he is concerned only with dying himself and entreats Paris to leave. Romeo says to Paris, "By heaven I love thee better than myself." He responded similarly to Tybalt's insults in Act III, Scene 1, "But [I] love thee better than thou canst devise."

After Paris is dead, Romeo realizes who Paris is and describes them both as the victims of fate: "One writ with me in sour misfortune's book." Paris is a noble suitor and defends Juliet's grave with his life. His death, like Mercutio's, is tragic in that he never knew the love shared by Romeo and Juliet.

Character Insight

Romeo's sudden sense of compassion for the dying Paris may be understandable. When Romeo courted Rosaline, he found her cold and unresponsive to his amorous desires. Like Romeo, Paris received little beyond polite conversation from Juliet; her love was entirely dedicated to Romeo. Like Romeo, Paris is a worthy suitor of good character and noble intent. The pain of an unrequited love is not foreign to Romeo, and the fact that Paris will die, like Mercutio, without enlightenment or exposure to true, transcendent, spiritual love catalyzes great compassion and sympathy in Romeo.

Character Insight

Rather than demonstrating weakness or a distracted mindset, Juliet's death indicates her dignity and strength of character. The Romans regarded stabbing as the most noble form of suicide. Juliet ignores the Friar's warnings and deliberately follows through with her vow to be with Romeo in death.

Thus the play concludes with the reconciliation of the families—a somewhat Pyrrhic triumph. As the originators of the feud stand amidst the dead bodies of their city's youth, the rift is healed. Romeo and Juliet have achieved spiritual reunion in death, and their lives will be memorialized in gold as witness to their sacrifice. The conclusion seems somewhat empty because Romeo and Juliet triumph in death—an ending that manifests the very essence of the tragedy itself. However, measuring the tragedy by the crude barometer of the moral lessons that the survivors learn seems obtuse. The tragedy can be appreciated in the context of the protagonists' understanding of their own lives. The soul of the tragedy is not constituted in the joy they had and lost; rather, the soul of the tragedy lies in the joy that could never last in this world.

Glossary

obsequies funeral rites.

cross to thwart.

mattock a tool for loosening the soil: it is like a pickax but has a flat, adz-shaped blade on one or both sides.

dear employment important purpose.

jealous suspicious.

conjuration solemn entreaty.

lantern an open or windowed structure on the roof of a building or in the upper part of a tower or the like, to admit light or air.

feasting presence presence chamber: the room in which a king or other person of rank or distinction formally receives guests.

keepers guards, as of prisoners.

a light'ning before death! Romeo refers to the belief that on the point of death the spirits were supposed to revive.

conduct that is, the poison.

unthrifty unlucky.

discoloured bloodstained.

churl a surly, ill-bred person.

rust corruption, decay.

descry detect.

let mischance be slave to patience submit to these unfortunate events with patience.

kill your joys kill your children and turn your joy to sorrow.

winking turning a blind eye to.

glooming peace peace overshadowed with grief.

CHARACTER ANALYSES

Juliet

Juliet, like Romeo, makes the transition from an innocent adolescent to responsible adult during the course of the play. In Juliet's case, however, there is a heightened sense that she has been forced to mature too quickly. The emphasis throughout the play on Juliet's youth, despite her growing maturity, establishes her as a tragic heroine.

Juliet is presented as quiet and obedient; however, she possesses an inner strength that enables her to have maturity beyond her years. When her mother suggests that she marry Paris because Paris is rich and good looking, Juliet responds: "I'll look to like, if looking liking move" (I.3.97).

When she meets and falls in love with Romeo, she is prepared to defy her parents and marry Romeo in secret. In Act III, Scene 5, Capulet demands his right as her father to marry her to Paris, threatening her with disinheritance and public shame.

Juliet, however, is resolute in her decision to die rather than enter into a false marriage: "If all else fail, myself have power to die" (III.5.244). At this point, when Juliet is most isolated from her family, even the Nurse betrays Juliet's trust by advising her to forget Romeo and comply with her father's wishes.

In her relationship with Romeo, Juliet is loving, witty, loyal, and strong. When Romeo and Juliet kiss at the feast, Juliet teases Romeo for using the popular imagery of love poetry to express his feelings and for kissing according to convention rather than from the heart: "You kiss by th' book" (I.5.110). This establishes a pattern for their relationship in which Juliet displays greater maturity, particularly in moments of great emotional intensity.

In the balcony scene of Act II, Scene 2, Juliet is aware of the foolhardiness of their love: "It is too rash, too unadvis'd, too sudden." This sense of rushing headlong accurately characterizes their love, yet despite her premonition, Juliet is the one who suggests later in the scene that they marry. Act III, Scene 2, marks Juliet's move toward sexual and emotional maturity when she anticipates the consummation of her marriage to Romeo. The lyrical language Juliet employs as she waits impatiently for the night to come underscores the intensity of her feelings:

> Spread thy close curtain, love-performing night,
> That runaway eyes may wink, and Romeo
> Leap to these arms untalk'd of and unseen.

The news of Tybalt's death initially produces conflicting feelings for Juliet because she's torn between her love for her husband and the loyalty she feels for Tybalt, her slain cousin: "Shall I speak ill of him that is my husband?" (III.2.98). Juliet's love for Romeo soon resolves the conflict:

> My husband lives, that Tybalt would have slain,
> And Tybalt's dead, that would have slain my husband.
> All this is comfort.
>
> (III.2.105–107)

Juliet's decision in Act IV to take the Friar's potion rather than enter into a bigamous marriage with Paris increases Juliet's stature as a tragic heroine. She reflects on the plan but prepares to face the dangers involved bravely: "My dismal scene I needs must act alone."

Romeo

During the course of the play, Romeo matures from adolescence to adulthood as a result of his love for Juliet and his unfortunate involvement in the feud, marking his development from a comic character to a tragic figure.

Romeo is initially presented as a *Petrarchan* lover, a man whose feelings of love aren't reciprocated by the lady he admires and who uses the poetic language of sonnets to express his emotions about his situation. Romeo's exaggerated language in his early speeches characterizes him as a young and inexperienced lover who is more in love with the concept of being in love than with the woman herself.

The play's emphasis on characters' eyes and the act of looking accords with Romeo's role as a blind lover who doesn't believe that there could be another lady more fair than his Rosaline. Romeo denies that he could be deluded by love, the "religion" of his eye. This zeal, combined with his rejection of Benvolio's advice to find another love to replace Rosaline, highlights Romeo's immaturity as a lover. Similar imagery creates a comic effect when Romeo falls in love at first sight with Juliet at the Capulet feast. When Romeo sees Juliet, he realizes the artificiality of his love for Rosaline: "Did my heart love till now? Forswear it, sight! / For I ne'er saw true beauty till this night" (I.5.52–53).

As the play progresses, Romeo's increasing maturity as a lover is marked by the change in his language. He begins to speak in blank verse as well as rhyme, which allows his language to sound less artificial and more like everyday language.

The fated destinies of Romeo and Juliet are foreshadowed throughout the play. Romeo's sense of foreboding as he makes his way to the Capulet feast anticipates his first meeting with Juliet:

> my mind misgives
> Some consequence yet hanging in the stars
> Shall bitterly begin his fearful date
>
> (I.4.106–107)

Romeo's role first as a melancholy lover in the opening scenes of the play and then as a Juliet's secret love is significant. Romeo belongs in a world defined by love rather than a world fractured by feud. Tybalt's death in Act III, Scene 1, brings about the clash between the private world of the lovers and the public world of the feud. Romeo is reluctant to fight Tybalt because they are now related through Romeo's marriage to Juliet.

When Tybalt kills Mercutio, however, Romeo (out of loyalty to his friend and anger at Tybalt's arrogance) kills Tybalt, thus avenging his friend's death. In one ill-fated moment, he placed his love of Juliet over his concern for Mercutio, and Mercutio was killed. Romeo then compounds the problem by placing his own feelings of anger over any concerns for Juliet by killing Tybalt.

Romeo's immaturity is again manifest later when he learns of his banishment. He lies on the floor of the Friar's cell, wailing and crying over his fate. When the nurse arrives, he clumsily attempts suicide. The Friar reminds him to consider Juliet and chides him for not thinking through the consequences of his actions for his wife.

The Friar then offers a course of action to follow, and Romeo becomes calm. Later, when Romeo receives the news of Juliet's death, he exhibits maturity and composure as he resolves to die. His only desire is to be with Juliet: "Well Juliet, I will lie with thee tonight" (V.1.36). His resolution is reflected in the violent image he uses to order Balthasar, his servant, to keep out of the tomb:

> The time and my intents are savage-wild,
> More fierce and more inexorable far
> Than empty tigers or the roaring sea.
>
> (V,3,37–40)

After killing Paris, Romeo remorsefully takes pity on him and fulfills Paris' dying wish to be laid next to Juliet. Romeo notes that both he and Paris are victims of fate and describes Paris as: "One writ with me in sour misfortune's book" (V.3.83) since Paris experienced an unreciprocated love from Juliet similar to Romeo's unrequited love for Rosaline. Romeo is also filled with compassion because he knows that Paris has died without understanding the true love that he and Juliet shared.

Romeo's final speech recalls the Prologue in which the "star-cross'd" lives of the lovers are sacrificed to end the feud:

> O here
> Will I set up my everlasting rest
> And shake the yoke of inauspicious stars
> From this world wearied flesh.
>
> (V.3.109–112)

The Nurse

The Nurse's key function within the play is to act as a go-between for Romeo and Juliet, and is the only other character besides Friar Laurence to know of their wedding. The Nurse, despite being a servant in the Capulet household, has a role equivalent to that of Juliet's mother and regards Juliet as her own daughter.

The Nurse's relationship with Juliet focuses attention on Juliet's age. In Juliet's first scene, the Nurse repeatedly asserts that Juliet has not yet had her 14th birthday. In contrast to Juliet's youth, the Nurse is old and enjoys complaining about her aches and pains. Juliet's frustration at having to rely upon the Nurse as her messenger is used to comic effect in Act II, Scene 5, when Juliet is forced to listen to the Nurse's ailments while trying to coax from her the news of her wedding plans:

The Nurse, like Mercutio, loves to talk at length. She often repeats herself, and her bawdy references to the sexual aspect of love set the idealistic love of Romeo and Juliet apart from the love described by other characters in the play. The Nurse doesn't share Juliet's idea of love; for her, love is a temporary and physical relationship, so she can't understand the intense and spiritual love Romeo and Juliet share. When the Nurse brings Juliet news of Romeo's wedding arrangements, she focuses on the pleasures of Juliet's wedding night, "I am the drudge, and toil in your delight, / But you shall bear the burden soon at night" (II.5.75–76).

This clash in outlook manifests itself when she advises Juliet to forget the banished Romeo and marry Paris, betraying Juliet's trust by advocating a false marriage:

> I think it best you married with the County.
> O, he's a lovely gentleman.
> Romeo's a dishclout to him.
>
> (III.5.218–220)

Juliet can't believe that the Nurse offers such a course of action after she praised Romeo and helped bring the couple together. The Nurse is ultimately subject to the whims of society. Her social position places her in the serving class—she is not empowered to create change around her. Her maternal instinct toward Juliet buoys her to aid Juliet in marrying Romeo; however, when Capulet becomes enraged, the Nurse retreats quickly into submission and urges Juliet to forget Romeo.

Mercutio

Mercutio, the witty skeptic, is a foil for Romeo, the young Petrarchan lover. Mercutio mocks Romeo's vision of love and the poetic devices he uses to express his emotions:

> Romeo, Humors! Madman! Passion! Lover!
> Appear thou in the likeness of a sigh,
> Speak but one rhyme and I am satisfied.
>
> (II.1.7–9)

Mercutio is an anti-romantic character who, like Juliet's Nurse, regards love as an exclusively physical pursuit. He advocates an adversarial concept of love that contrasts sharply with Romeo's idealized notion of romantic union. In Act I, Scene 4, when Romeo describes his love for Rosaline using the image of love as a rose with thorns, Mercutio mocks this conventional device by punning bawdily:

> If love be rough with you, be rough with love;
> Prick love for pricking and you beat love down.
>
> (I,4,27–28)

The Queen Mab speech in Act I, Scene 4, displays Mercutio's eloquence and vivid imagination, while illustrating his cynical side. Mercutio, unlike Romeo, doesn't believe that dreams can act as portents. Fairies predominate in the dream world Mercutio presents, and dreams are merely the result of the anxieties and desires of those who sleep.

Mercutio's speech, while building tension for Romeo's first meeting with Juliet at the Capulet ball, indicates that although Mercutio is Romeo's friend, he can never be his confidant. As the play progresses, Mercutio remains unaware of Romeo's love and subsequent marriage to Juliet.

When Mercutio hears of Tybalt's challenge to Romeo, he is amused because he regards Romeo as a lover whose experience of conflict is limited to the world of love. So he scornfully asks: "And is he such a man to encounter Tybalt?" (II.3.16–17). Mercutio seems to exist outside the two dominant spheres of Verona because he takes neither the world of love nor the feud seriously. However, Mercutio, like Tybalt, is quick-tempered and they are both ready to draw their swords at the slightest provocation.

Mercutio is antagonistic toward Tybalt by suggesting that Tybalt is a follower of the new trends in swordsmanship, which he regards as effeminate. Like Tybalt, Mercutio has a strong sense of honor and can't understand Romeo's refusal to fight Tybalt, calling it, "O calm, dishonorable, vile submission" (III.1.72). Mercutio demonstrates his loyalty and courage when he takes up Tybalt's challenge to defend his friend's name.

The humor with which Mercutio describes his fatal wound confirms his appeal as a comic character: "No 'tis not so deep as a well, nor so wide as a church door, but 'tis enough, 'twill serve" (III.1.94—95). Mercutio's death creates sympathy for Romeo's enraged, emotional reaction in avenging his friend's death. His death marks a distinct turning point in the play as tragedy begins to overwhelm comedy, and the fates of the protagonists darken.

Friar Laurence

Friar Laurence is presented as a holy man who is trusted and respected by the other characters. The Friar's role as the friend and advisor to Romeo and Juliet highlights the conflict between parents and their children within the play. The centrality of the Friar's role suggests a notable failure of parental love. Romeo and Juliet can't tell their parents of their love because of the quarrel between the two families.

In their isolation, Romeo and Juliet turn to the Friar who can offer neutral advice. At first, the Friar can't believe how quickly Romeo has abandoned Rosaline and fallen in love with Juliet, so he reminds Romeo of the suddenness of his decisions. The Friar uses the formal language of rhyme and proverbs to stress the need for caution to Romeo. However, he agrees to marry Romeo and Juliet in the hope that their marriage will heal the rift between the Montagues and the Capulets. His decision to marry the lovers is well-meaning but indicates that he has been naive in his assessment of the feud and hasn't reflected on the implications of Romeo and Juliet's clandestine marriage.

The conflict between youth and old age also manifests itself in the Friar's relationship with Romeo and Juliet. When Friar Lawrence tries to soothe Romeo's grief at the news of his banishment with rational argument, Romeo quickly responds that if the Friar were young and in love, he wouldn't accept such advice any better.

The Friar's knowledge of plants—especially their dual qualities to heal and hurt—play an important role in the action that follows. His attempts to heal the feud by reversing nature—causing Juliet's "death" in order to bring about acceptance of her life with Romeo is notably *unnatural*. The Friar must extricate Juliet from the tomb in order to save her life—another reversal of nature. This use of nature for unnatural purposes precipitates many of the consequences leading to the tragic conclusion of the play. Ultimately, the Friar acts distinctly human—he flees the tomb and abandons Juliet.

CRITICAL ESSAYS

The Role of Comic Characters in the Tragedy of *Romeo and Juliet*

Shakespeare uses Mercutio and the Nurse to explore the relationship between comedy and tragedy in *Romeo and Juliet*. These characters, in their comic roles, serve as foils for Romeo and Juliet by highlighting the couple's youth and innocence as well as the pure and vulnerable quality of their love.

Mercutio, Romeo's quick-tempered, witty friend, links the comic and violent action of the play. He is initially presented as a playful rogue who possesses both a brilliant comic capacity and an opportunistic, galvanized approach to love. Later, Mercutio's death functions as a turning point for the action of the play. In death, he becomes a tragic figure, shifting the play's direction from comedy to tragedy.

Mercutio's first appearance in Act I, Scene 4, shows Romeo and his friend to be of quite opposite characters. Mercutio mocks Romeo as a helpless victim of an overzealous, undersatisfied love. Romeo describes his love for Rosaline using the clichéd image of the rose with thorns to stress the pain of his unrequited love.

Mercutio ridicules Romeo as a fashionable, Petrarchan lover for his use of conventional poetic imagery. He puns lewdly, "If love be rough with you, be rough with love; / Prick love for pricking and you beat love down." Whereas the naïve Romeo is in love with the idea of being in love and devoted to the distant Rosaline, Mercutio is a predatory lover, hunting for objectified, female prey. His bawdy wit thus sets up Romeo to take the role of the innocent tragic hero.

When Mercutio delivers his Queen Mab speech (also in Act I, Scene 4), he again characterizes Romeo as a clueless romantic for believing that dreams portend future events. Dismissing Romeo's Petrarchan outlook, Mercutio presents his vision of a fantasy world in which dreams are the products of people's fleshly desires. The speech reflects both Mercutio's eloquent wit and his aggressive disposition. In his speech, the comic activities of the mischievous fairies are juxtaposed with the violent images of a soldier's dream:

> Sometime she driveth o'er a soldier's neck
> And then dreams he of cutting foreign throats,
> Of breaches, ambuscados, Spanish blades . . . .

(I.iv.82-84)

After falling in love with Juliet, Romeo cannot confide in his anti-romantic friend, so Mercutio never discovers Romeo's love for Juliet. Mercutio's ignorance of Romeo's new love, although potentially comical, propels him to the fatal fight with Tybalt in Act III, Scene 1. Mercutio's death enables Shakespeare to develop him as a tragic figure and alter the trajectory of the play from a comic to a tragic course.

Mercutio's final speech employs dark comedy to illustrate the tragic significance of the latest violence. After being stabbed by Tybalt, he admits his wound is fatal. Mercutio puns, "Ask for me tomorrow and you shall find me a grave man." Mercutio dies frustrated and angry—shocked and in disbelief that his fate is upon him. Until and even in the midst of that moment, his ignorance of the underlying forces that brought him to such an untimely end provides much of the ironic humor for the play.

In Act II, Scene 1, Mercutio and Benvolio's search for Romeo after the feast provides a comic interlude between Romeo and Juliet's first meeting and the famous balcony scene in Act II, Scene 2, juxtaposing two very different and conflicting attitudes to love. Mercutio and Benvolio call to Romeo, who has climbed into Capulet's orchard in the hope of seeing Juliet again. Mercutio's teasing is ironic because he is unaware that Romeo has fallen in love with Juliet and mistakenly invokes images of Rosaline to call him:

> I conjure thee by Rosaline's bright eyes,
> By her high forehead and her scarlet lip,
> By her fine foot, straight leg, and quivering thigh,
> And the demesnes that there adjacent lie.

(II.i.17-21)

Mercutio's coarse physical imagery and sexual jokes contrast sharply with Romeo's religious imagery for love. Romeo describes Juliet as "bright angel" and "dear saint." Shakespeare uses Mercutio's cynical attitude to distinguish Romeo and Juliet's love as innocent, spiritual, and intense. Because the audience is aware that Mercutio's speech falls on deaf ears, Mercutio's speech illustrates that the Romeo, the lovestruck youth, has begun to mature in his outlook on life and love.

Like Mercutio, Juliet's Nurse views love as a purely sexual and temporary relationship, as opposed to Romeo and Juliet's love which is presented as fragile and eternal. The Nurse's bawdy humor is less sophisticated than Mercutio's. Her comedy comes from the Nurse's misunderstanding of language and her habit of repeating herself, rather than clever wordplay. For example, in Act I, Scene 3, the Nurse exasperates Lady Capulet, who has come to talk to Juliet of the proposed marriage to Paris, with her repeated and unrelated assertions that Juliet is only 13 years old.

Likewise, when the Nurse laughingly recounts the lewd joke her husband made when Juliet fell over learning to walk—"Thou wilt fall backward when thou hast more wit"—her earthy humor contrasts with Juliet's adolescent innocence, while simultaneously pointing to Juliet's sexual development from a girl to a woman. Reflecting on the sensual pleasures that await Juliet on her wedding night, the Nurse puns about the likely consequence of pregnancy for her young charge: "I am the drudge, and toil in your delight, / But you shall bear the burden soon at night."

The Nurse's preoccupation with sexual love prevents her from understanding the nature of Juliet's love for Romeo. Even though she fully understands that Juliet is being bartered like livestock, she cannot see that any other social fate could exist for women. So, in Act III, Scene 5, the Nurse advises Juliet to forget Romeo and marry Paris when Capulet demands it. This development of her character further isolates the couple and fuels the tragic consequences of their elevated love. Thus, while the Nurse drives some of the most comedic scenes in the play, within her comic commentaries are woven the subtler threads of tragedy created by enslavement to social conventions.

Shakespeare uses the comic roles of Mercutio and the Nurse to develop the roles of Romeo and Juliet as young tragic lovers. Prior to Tybalt and Mercutio's deaths, the Nurse had served primarily as comic relief. After Mercutio dies, the Nurse's comic role changes to a less sympathetic one—helping to shift the focus to the tragic plight of Romeo and Juliet. Both comic characters' rejection of the ideal of love shared by Romeo and Juliet emphasizes the vulnerable quality of that love and its inability to survive in the world of the play.

Critical analysis of setting in the opening scenes of Luhrmann's film, *Romeo + Juliet*

To assess Baz Luhrmann's use of setting in his film, *Romeo + Juliet*, we can begin by contrasting the film with the play as it was originally performed in the 16th-century theatre. The key difference between the manner in which the film and the play deal with location is that the film is primarily an image-intensive medium that can visually show the audience the locale. Shakespearean drama, on the other hand, was written to be heard as an auditory experience.

Shakespeare's audience referred to going to *hear* a play rather than see it, emphasizing that the Elizabethan theater was an aural rather than visual experience. On stage, the characters described the setting in their speeches. The actor's words had to convey all necessary information about plot, characters, and setting because the action took place on a bare, open-air stage, with only a few props and limited costumes. The plays were performed in the afternoon, and the playhouses did not have the advantages of lighting or special effects. For example, the scenes which take place at night make repeated references to objects associated with darkness, such as the moon, stars, and artificial sources of light, such as lamps and torches, to help create a sense of atmosphere and setting.

The Prologue sets the scene in both the play and the film. In *Romeo + Juliet*, Luhrmann presents the Prologue as a news bulletin that gives the events a feeling of immediacy—the urgency of an on-the-spot news report. The news broadcaster has replaced the Shakespearean Chorus for a modern audience while retaining the Chorus's function of providing commentary on events before they happen.

Luhrmann emphasizes the setting as the Prologue ends. The camera zooms forward to scenes of Verona, with the words "IN FAIR VERONA" flashing on the screen. Luhrmann presents Verona as a modern city, dominated by scenes of chaotic urban violence. Aerial shots pan across the cityscape as police cars and helicopters dart about, and human casualties are strewn across the ground. Watching impassively is an enormous statue of Jesus. These opening shots of a city divided by violence sets the scene for the subsequent action of the film.

These vivid location shots perform the same function as the Prologue for Shakespeare's first audience. A 16th-century playgoer would have associated the hot climate, fiery, passionate nature of the people, and strong sense of family honor with the Italian locale. By comparison, the film puts the viewer in the midst of the strife-torn city infected with crime and decay. The film uses these graphic images of violence to communicate the setting to the audience.

In the film, the first six lines of the Prologue are repeated as a voice-over to accompany more news footage covering the latest outbreak of violence caused by the feud. Media coverage of the civil unrest stresses how the feud affects the entire city. As the voice reads, "Two houses both alike in dignity," the camera pulls back to reveal the photographs of both families on the front page of the city's newspaper. The next two lines of the Prologue are displayed as newspaper headlines and juxtaposed with clips of riot police attempting to restore order on the streets. The media's presentation of the feud illustrates the impact of the "ancient grudge" on the city while importing the play's introductory content in a format familiar to a modern audience.

Both the Prologue and the opening scene of the film use setting to establish the opposing parties. In the film version, we see how the two opposed families dominate Verona Beach from the way skyscrapers bearing the names Montague and Capulet overshadow the city's horizon. Luhrmann follows this image with photographs of the two families on the front of the newspaper separated by a photograph of the statue of Jesus. The repeated focus on the Jesus statue and other religious icons comments on how religion, like the law, is no longer an effective means of maintaining peace and harmony in modern society. Shakespeare's disregard of religion as a force in maintaining social order may not have been so blatant as Luhrmann's treatment in the film. Shakespeare presents the Friar as a well-intentioned character despite the Friar's impotence to affect the tragic outcome of the action.

In the opening scene, the city of Verona is renamed Verona Beach, evoking America's famous city on the beach, Miami. The film draws on pop-culture images such as those from *Miami Vice*, which depicted both urban glamour and crime. Luhrmann clearly distinguishes the downtown area from the beach. He associates the city with the violence of the feud and the idyllic beach with love and peace.

The film illustrates these opposing forces through the use of a fire and water motif. In both the news footage and an encounter between the Montagues and Capulets at a gas station, flames repeatedly engulf the surroundings. "Fiery" Tybalt in particular seems to have a distinctly combustible effect on his surroundings. Romeo and Juliet, in contrast, are connected with water throughout the film. We first see Romeo on the beach looking to the ocean. Later, Romeo and Juliet see each other for the first time through a fish tank, and the famous balcony scene takes place in a swimming pool.

The beach, through its connection with the sea, becomes a place for change as opposed to the concrete, unchanging nature of the city. Luhrmann uses the beach as the place where the worlds of love and conflict clash when peaceable Romeo encounters "fiery" Tybalt. Moments later, Mercutio is killed there, symbolizing a loss of innocence, a violation of purity, and a defamation of a natural order.

Luhrmann places a huge Elizabethan stage on the beach to acknowledge the film's awareness of its Shakespearean heritage. The stage also provides several characters an alternative vehicle for expressing their emotional development, or lack thereof. Luhrmann presents a youthful, immature Romeo seated on stage, delivering his Rosaline-inspired "O brawling love" speech as a voice-over. The speech sounds stilted, stiff, and staged as though Romeo were a young, incompetent actor who merely recites his lines mechanically without understanding their meaning.

Luhrmann chooses a modern city as the setting for his film adaptation of *Romeo and Juliet* to present a chaotic urban world familiar to a 20th-century cinema audience. The media coverage of the feud makes the play's events familiar to a modern audience as they watch violent video of the chaos on the streets of Verona Beach and are drawn into the feud-ravaged world of the film. The updated and renamed Verona Beach is a clever mechanism by which peaceful and violent worlds collide.

CliffsNotes Review

Use this CliffsNotes Review to test your understanding of the original text, and reinforce what you've learned in the book. After you work through the review and essay questions, identify the quote section, and the fun and useful practice projects, you're well on your way to understanding a comprehensive and meaningful interpretation of Shakespeare's *Romeo and Juliet*.

Review Questions

1. Love manifests itself in a multitude of ways in the play. Compare and contrast Romeo's love for Rosaline with Romeo's love for Juliet. Consider love as it exists in the Capulet household. How does love operate between Lord and Lady Capulet, Juliet, the Nurse, and Tybalt?

2. Some readers consider the final scene in which both Romeo and Juliet die to be triumphant. In addition to the families being reconciled, how is the final scene triumphant?

3. Consider Lord Capulet's personality. How do his moods change and why? How does these mood swings affect Juliet, and how do they affect the course of the play?

4. Compare and contrast Romeo's reaction to the news of his banishment with Juliet's reaction.

5. Examine the role of Escalus, the Prince, as the play's figure of authority. How far is he to blame for what happens?

6. Some critics have said that Shakespeare had to kill Mercutio as he was becoming such a compelling characters that he detracted from Romeo and Juliet. Do you agree? Why or why not?

7. Light in its various forms recurrs throughout the play. How does light mirror the action? How does the author use light to describe the characters and the changes they undergo?

8. As the Friar picks his herbs, he tells us that nature's tomb is also her womb and that what dies gives birth to new life. How do the Friar's words anticipate upcoming events? Do you think that the Friar proactively creates events that follow, or does he react to situations that are beyond his control? Explain.

9. Juliet is a very young girl; however, she shoulders a great deal of responsibility and manages a series of very difficult situations. Discuss Juliet's maturity level and compare it to Romeo's. Compare Juliet early in the play with Juliet later in the play. How has she changed? When did she change? Why did those changes occur?

10. The first Prologue describes Romeo and Juliet as, "A pair of star-cross'd lovers." Examine the way Shakespeare uses cosmic imagery in the play to emphasize the connection between Romeo and Juliet and their tragic deaths.

11. Shakespeare makes the plot of *Romeo and Juliet* rely on the delivery of crucial messages. Explain the importance of these various messages and the problems with the messengers.

12. Dreams often play an important part in Shakespearean dramas. At several points in the play, the characters have dreams. Sometimes they interpret them correctly, and other times they don't. Discuss these instances and how the characters' reactions to those dreams affect the action in the play. How do the characters interpret or misinterpret their dreams?

13. The feud between the families seems to be an ever-present concern for the characters. How does the feud drive the action of the play. How do the various characters manifest the feud?

Questions and Answers

1. Who Kills Tybalt?

   a. Mercutio

   b. Romeo

   c. Benvolio

   d. Paris

2. What does Juliet place by her bedside as she takes the sleeping potion?

   a. A prayer book

   b. A sword

   c. Romeo's picture

   d. A dagger

3. Who is described as "Sharp misery had worn him to the bones"?

   a. Capulet

   b. Romeo

   c. Apothecary

   d. Mercutio

4. Who is the last person to see Juliet alive?

   a. Romeo

   b. Friar Laurence

   c. Capulet

   d. The Nurse

5. Why doesn't Romeo's mother accompany her husband to the tomb in the final act?

   a. She was sick

   b. She was searching for Romeo in Mantua

   c. She was dead

   d. She was estranged from the family

Answers: (1) b. (2) d. (3) c. (4) b. (5) c.

Identify the Quote

Identify the speaker and importance of the quote in the context of the entire play.

1. O brawling love, O loving hate.

2. A crutch, a crutch. Why call you for a sword?

3. But soft! What light through yonder window breaks?

4. What's in a name? That which we call a rose / By any other name would smell as sweet.

5. Arise fair sun, and kill the envious moon

6. Like violent delights have violent ends / And in their triumph die, like fire and powder, / Which, as they kiss, consume.

7. No, 'tis not so deep as a well, nor so wide as a church door; but 'tis enough, 'twill serve. Ask for me tomorrow, and you shall find me a grave man.

8. O I am fortune's fool!

9. Then, window, let day in, and let life out.

10. My poverty but not my will consents.

Answers: (1) In Act I, Scene 1, Romeo laments his unrequited love for Rosaline. (2) Lady Capulet, in Act I, Scene 1, scoffs at her husband's impulsive desire to join a street fight. (3) In Act II, Scene 2, Romeo is dazzled by Juliet when he sees her on her balcony. (4) In Act II, Scene 2, Juliet laments the arbitrary distinctions the Capulets and Montagues attach to their names. (5) Romeo, in Act II, Scene 2, expresses his desire for Juliet (the sun) and his abandonment of his love for Rosaline (the moon). (6) In Act II, Scene 6, the Friar warns that haste in matters of love may lead to disasterous results. (7) Mercutio, in Act III, Scene 1, jokes after being mortally wounded by Tybalt. (8) Romeo cries out in frustration in Act III, Scene 1 when he realizes that his impulsive behavior cost Tybalt his life and may have cost him Juliet as well. (9) In Act III, Scene 5, Juliet bids farewell to Romeo as he escapes through her window following their wedding night. (10) The Apothecary consents to illegally sell Romeo poison in Act V, Scene 1.

CliffsNotes Resource Center

Books

BASSNETT, SUSAN. "Wayward Sons and Daughters: Romeo and Juliet, A Midsummer Night's Dream and Henry IV, Part 1." in *Shakespeare: The Elizabethan Plays.* Macmillan Press Ltd., London. 1993.

BOAGEY, ERIC. *Starting Shakespeare.* Collins Educational, London. 1983.

BROOKE, NICHOLAS. *Shakespeare's Early Tragedies.* Methuen & Co Ltd., London. 1968.

HARRISON, G.B. *Introducing Shakespeare.* Penguin Books Ltd., London. (1939) 1966.

LEVENSON, JILL L. *Shakespeare in Performance. Romeo and Juliet.* Manchester University Press, Manchester. 1987.

———, Shakespeare, William. The New Cambridge Shakespeare *Romeo and Juliet.* ed. G. Blakemore Evans. Cambridge University Press, Cambridge. 1996.

Internet

The Shakespeare Resource Center, www.bardweb.net/ plays.html— J.M. Pressley edits this site which offers information on the author, his plays, commentary, Elizabethan England, Shakespeare's language, and a host of other topics. Also includes links to other valuable resources.

The Shakespeare Classroom, www.jetlink.net/~massij/ shakes/ index.shtml—Professor Massi created this award winning site which is aimed at students studying Shakespeare in high school or college. There is a useful section with study questions on individual plays, including *Romeo and Juliet*, together with a page offering points to think about when watching a Shakespeare film. The editor J.M Massi teaches Shakespeare at Washington State University and has compiled a page with the most frequently asked questions about Shakespeare and his work. Students are also able to e-mail the editor with their questions.

Surfing with the Bard, www.ulen.com/shakespeare/—Amy Ulen has compiled a fun collection of sites, resources, and commentary on Shakespeare's works. It includes chat rooms for discussion, teacher resources, student guides, and reviews.

An Introduction to Shakespeare's Life and Times, web.uvic.ca/ shakespeare/Library/SLT/— Professor Michael Best of the University of Victoria compiles a comprehensive collection of information on Shakespeare including the history, politics, ideas, art, music, stage, and drama of the time.

Next time you're on the Internet, don't forget to drop by www.cliffsnotes.com. We've created an online Resource Center that you can use today, tomorrow, and beyond

Films and Other Recordings

William Shakespeare's *Romeo + Juliet*, dir. Baz Luhrmann. With Leonardo DiCaprio and Claire Danes. Twentieth Century Fox Film Corporation, 1997. 115 mins.

Romeo and Juliet, dir. Franco Zeferrelli. With Olivia Hussey and Leonard Whiting. Paramount Pictures Corporation, 1968. 132 mins.

West Side Story, dir. Robert Wise and Jerome Robbins. With Natalie Wood. Warner Home Video, (1961) 1986. 147 mins.

Romeo and Juliet, With Patrick Ryecart, Rebecca Saire, Alan Rickman and Sir John Gielgud. BBC Enterprises, 1988. 188 mins.

Audiotape

Shakespeare, William. *Romeo and Juliet*. BBC Radio 3 full cast production. With Sophie Dahl and Douglas Henshall. BBC Worldwide Ltd, 1999. 180 mins. The tapes are accompanied by a booklet which contains a scene by scene synopsis, character analysis, and an essay by the producer on his interpretation of the play.

Shakespeare, William. *Romeo and Juliet*. Harper Collins Audio Books. With Albert Finney, Claire Bloom, and Dame Edith Evans. Caedmon 1961. 165 mins.

Index

NOTES

NOTES

Check Out the All-New CliffsNotes Guides

TECHNOLOGY TOPICS

PERSONAL FINANCE TOPICS

CAREER TOPICS